Law and Justice in Small Island Developing States

This book systematically identifies the challenges and features of law and development, as faced by small island developing states (SIDS). The book contextualizes this through the case study of Niue, a self-governing state in free association with New Zealand since 1974.

The book surveys literature to discuss the features and vulnerabilities of SIDS and the challenges of law and development in these contexts. It then analyses the case of Niue and covers the current situation regarding the rule of law and access to justice on the island. It further analyses the impact of COVID-19 on the fragility of the Niuean justice system. The book considers the case study of Niue and discusses how rule of law assistance is rendered in the Pacific region. It discusses previous law and justice projects implemented by international organizations and bilateral donors, and recommends ways forward to improve human rights and access to justice in these vulnerable states.

This book will appeal to scholars of law and development, rule of law, and Pacific law. It will also provide a comprehensive resource on Niuean law for residents and legal practitioners.

Mana Takahashi is Associate Professor of Faculty of Global Liberal Arts, Kanda University of International Studies in Japan. She received her PhD in Comparative Law from Nagoya University in 2018. Her research interests are law and development, global governance, and Oceania Regional Studies.

Kahealani Sinahemana Hekau is a law practitioner and member of the Niue Assembly. She has contributed to the books, *South Pacific Land Systems* and *Legal Systems of the Pacific – Introducing Sixteen Gems* and published in the *Comparative Law Journal of the Pacific* on governance.

Routledge Studies in Asian Law

National Identity and Japanese Revisionism
Abe Shinzō's Vision of a Beautiful Japan and its Limits
Michal Kolmaš

Constitutional Remedies in Asia
Edited by Po Jen Yap

Chinese Legal Culture and Constitutional Order
Shiping Hua

Land Law and Disputes in Asia
In Search of an Alternative for Development
Edited by Brian Z. Tamanaha, Narufumi Kadomatsu and Yuka Kaneko

China's Foreign Investment Legal Regime
Progress and Limitations
Yuwen Li and Cheng Bian

Philosophy of Law in Korea
Acceptance, Engagement and Social Change
Jeong-Oh Kim, Hak-Tai Kim, Joon-Seok Park, Dong-Ryong Shin

The Law and Regulation of Public Health
Global Perspectives on Hong Kong
Eric C. Ip

State Administrative Law in Indonesia
M. Zaenul Muttaqin

Stem Cell Governance and Ethics
Mohammad Firdaus Bin Abdul Aziz

Law and Justice in Small Island Developing States
Lessons from Niue – Tutonuhia he tagata Niue
Mana Takahashi and Kahealani Sinahemana Hekau

For more information about this series, please visit: https://www.routledge.com/asianstudies/series/RSIAL

Law and Justice in Small Island Developing States

Lessons from Niue – Tutonuhia he tagata Niue

Mana Takahashi and
Kahealani Sinahemana Hekau

Routledge
Taylor & Francis Group
LONDON AND NEW YORK

First published 2026
by Routledge
4 Park Square, Milton Park, Abingdon, Oxon OX14 4RN

and by Routledge
605 Third Avenue, New York, NY 10158

Routledge is an imprint of the Taylor & Francis Group, an informa business

British Library Cataloguing-in-Publication Data
A catalogue record for this book is available from the British Library

Library of Congress Cataloging-in-Publication Data
Names: Takahashi, Mana (Author of Law and
Justice in Small Island
Developing States) author | Hekau, Kahealani Sinahemana author
Title: Law and justice in Small Island Developing States: lessons from
Niue / Mana Takahashi, Kahealani Sinahemana Hekau.
Description: Abingdon, Oxon [UK]; New York, NY:
Routledge, 2025. |
Series: Routledge studies in Asian law |
Includes bibliographical references and index.
Identifiers: LCCN 2025039943 | ISBN 9781032956015
hardback | ISBN
9781032956022 paperback | ISBN 9781003585688 ebook
Subjects: LCSH: Justice, Administration of–Niue |
Law–Niue | Rule of law–Niue | COVID-19 Pandemic,
2020-2023–Niue–Influence
Classification: LCC KWA34 .T35 2025 |
DDC 347.96–dc23/eng/20250828
LC record available at https://lccn.loc.gov/2025039943

ISBN: 9781032956015 (hbk)
ISBN: 9781032956022 (pbk)
ISBN: 9781003585688 (ebk)

DOI: 10.4324/9781003585688

Typeset in Galliard
by Deanta Global Publishing Services, Chennai, India

Contents

Acknowledgements

We would like to express our sincere gratitude to everyone who cooperated in the writing of this book, *Law and Justice in Small Island Developing States: Lessons from Niue – Tutonuhia he tagata Niue.*

Portions of this book are based on previously published work. We would like to thank the respective publishers for their permission to reproduce the following materials:

Chapter 4 is a revised version of an article by Mana Takahashi, "Unpacking Fragile Access to Justice in a Small Island State Amidst Global Pandemic: Narratives from Experiences of Niue, the Rock of Polynesia," originally published in *Law and Development Review*, vol. 18, no. 2 (2025), pp. 429–460.

Chapter 5 is also a revised version of an article by Mana Takahashi, "Thinking About a Judicial System for 'Leave No One Behind' in the Era of Anthropocene: A Context of Addressing SDGs Goal 16 in the Pacific Small Island States," originally published in *Global Communication Studies*, vol. 14 (2025), pp. 105–127. The original version is written in Japanese. This work was supported by the project titled "Interdisciplinary Approaches to Sustainable Development Goals (SDGs)" funded by the Global Communication Institute, Kanda University of International Studies.

These chapters have been revised and expanded for the purposes of this book.

We would also like to acknowledge the interviewees and practitioners who kindly agreed to participate in interviews for this research project.

We are deeply indebted to Emeritus Professor Tony Angelo, Faculty of Law at the Victoria University of Wellington, whose guidance and encouragement were invaluable throughout this project. Without his support, this work would not have been possible.

Mana would like to express her sincere gratitude to Emeritus Professor Yoshiharu Matsuura, Graduate School of Law at Nagoya University, for his insightful feedback and ongoing support. Thank you so much to Mana's wonderful colleagues at Kanda University of International Studies

(KUIS), especially those in the Faculty of Global Liberal Arts, for their intellectual inspiration, encouragement, and mentorship.

Kahealani is grateful to her Mom, Maihetoe Hekau and her family of Aliutu, Alofi South for their constant love and support. She acknowledges her colleagues Hon. Crossley Tatui of the Niue Cabinet and Hon. Tingika Elikana of the Cook Islands Cabinet for their wise counsels and thoughts.

This work was supported by the Research Grant Programme (2024–2027), funded by the KDDI Foundation.

We wish to acknowledge the editorial team at Routledge. We would particularly like to thank Kendrick Loo and Chelsea Low for their kind help and guidance.

Lastly, our heartfelt thanks go to our families and friends in Niue, Japan, and the world, whose support and love made this journey possible. Fakaaue lahi and Arigatou Gozaimasu!

1 Introduction

Mana Takahashi

1.1 The Rule of Law in the Context of Small Island Developing States (SIDS)

The Human Development Index (HDI), which was released by the United Nations Development Programme (UNDP) in 2020, provided a wake-up call for people living in a global society. The HDI is a comprehensive assessment of the state of economic and social development in each country and has been published annually by the UNDP since 1990.[1] The HDI, which has been rising steadily since 1990, showed that the world's economic and social conditions were improving annually, development was progressing, and people were becoming healthier and wealthier.[2] However, the figures released in 2020 showed a significant deterioration for the first time since 1990, indicating that the global development situation was "going backwards." A major influence on this situation was the global pandemic of COVID-19, and it has been noted that among the changes that have occurred in global society is a growing sense of anxiety in people's minds that their security is being threatened, or "loss of human security."[3] In this context, the following reference was made in the UNDP's Special Report for 2022:[4]

> In the background of the human development–human security disconnect looms the Anthropocene, the age of humans disrupting planetary processes.

We are currently living in the era of the Anthropocene. The Anthropocene, meaning "the age of mankind," is a new age category that was proposed by German chemist Paul J. Crutzen and American ecologist Eugene F. Stoermer and refers geologically to the Holocene of the Cenozoic

1 UNDP, "Human Development Index (HDI)."
2 UNDP, *New Threats to Human Security in the Anthropocene* (2022), p. 13.
3 *Ibid.*
4 *Ibid.*, p. 3.

DOI: 10.4324/9781003585688-1

Quaternary.[5] This means an era of "anthropocentricity," in which human activities affect the Earth's ecosystems, climate, and other aspects of life and leave lasting traces of their impact. As a result, various events occurring on Earth, such as climate change, loss of biodiversity, and increases in man-made chemicals, have correspondingly had a compounding effect on human security. This situation can be seen as a result of the industrial and economic activities of people aiming for "development" in global society, where globalization and industrialization have advanced since the end of World War II.

How have "legal" systems and human rights been affected by these anthropogenic global changes? How can the law protect people in the era of the Anthropocene?

Adelman notes the following regarding "law and development" in the era of the Anthropocene: although law is not so much affected by the context of unsustainable development, nor does it have a direct effect on environmental crises and problems, effective legal institutions and governance systems are essential for sustainability and climate justice.[6] In other words, the existence of legal systems does not of itself act on climate change or the global environment; however, they significantly affect people's behaviour and the establishment of social order, and the changes brought about by these systems can create "sustainable" conditions if they function efficiently. Conversely, the legal system can also function as a stable protection of the rights of every person living on earth from the changes in the earth brought about by human actions and their unequal effects.

The rule of law is a significant and fundamental concept. The United Nations refers to the rule of law as "fundamental to international peace and security and political stability; to achieve economic and social progress and development; and to protect people's rights and fundamental freedoms," and it is strongly interrelated with development.[7] The World Justice Program defines the rule of law similarly but more tangibly as "a durable system of laws, institutions, norms, and community commitment that delivers four universal principles: accountability, just law, open government, and accessible and impartial justice."[8] According to Zurn et al., the rule of law is also an ancient concept, but it has changed over time,

5 Atsuko Shigihara and Nanako Shimizu, "Hitoshinsei no Heiwagaku" (in Japanese), *Heiwa Kenkyu*, 58 (2023), pp. i–viii.

6 Sam Adelman, "Beyond Development: Towards Sustainability and Climate Justice in the Anthropocene," in Sam Adelman and Abdul Paliwala (eds), *The Limits of Law and Development* (New York: Routledge, 2021), p. 66.

7 United Nations and the Rule of Law, "What Is the Rule of Law?"

8 World Justice Project, "What Is the Rule of Law?"

influenced by international and transnational governance.[9] Montoya and Ponce noted that there are two principal conceptions of the rule of law: formalists' "thin" definition focusing on procedures and whether rules exist and scrutinizing whether those rules are followed by all, including sovereigns, as well as the government, who are thus bound by predictable rules; and a substantive "thick" definition focusing on certain rights that are seen to be fundamental to the rule of law and incorporating adherence to normative standards of rights, fairness, and equity.[10] They also explained that there is a variety of definitions of the rule of law, but all consider the rule of law in terms of its goals and outcomes and distinguish it from "rule by law."[11]

Achieving the rule of law is a global goal. The United Nations has stated the importance of a strengthened rule of law-based society to achieve global goals such as those in the 2030 Agenda for Sustainable Development.[12] The context of building inclusive institutions and ensuring justice in society is addressed in the Sustainable Development Goals (SDGs) Goal 16: promote peaceful and inclusive societies for sustainable development; provide access to justice for all; and build effective, accountable, and inclusive institutions at all levels.[13] In the current global society, rule of law assistance has been developed in various forms for rule of law promotion, involving a variety of actors, including international organizations, government agencies, non-governmental organizations (NGOs), and civil society.[14]

On the other hand, "regression from the rule of law" has appeared worldwide in recent years. Montoya and Ponce conducted a large quantitative analysis of the global rule of law situation for 2015–2022 with the *Rule of Law Index* by the World Justice Program and reported that the rule of law is weakened by a weakening of limitations on the exercise of

9 Michael Zürn, André Nolkaemper, and Randall Peerenboom, "Rule of Law Dynamics in an Era of International and Transnational Governance," in Michael Zürn, André Nolkaemper, and Randall Peerenboom (eds), *Rule of Law Dynamics* (New York: Cambridge University Press, 2012), pp. 1–4.

10 Maria Montoya and Alejandro Ponce, "Rule-of-Law Backsliding: Where, How, and Why," in Gregory Shaffer and Wayne Sandholtz (eds), *The Rule of Law Under Pressure: A Transnational Challenge* (New York: Cambridge University Press, 2025), pp. 115–116.

11 *Ibid.*, p. 118.

12 United Nations and the Rule of Law, *supra* note 7. United Nations General Assembly, *A/RES/70/1 Transforming Our World: The 2030 Agenda for Sustainable Development* (October 21, 2015).

13 United Nations General Assembly, *ibid.*

14 Frank Schimmelfennig, "A Comparison of the Rule of Law Promotion Policies of Major Western Powers," in Michael Zürn, André Nolkaemper, and Randall Peerenboom (eds), *Rule of Law Dynamics* (New York: Cambridge University Press, 2012), pp. 113–114; pp. 133–134.

state power and a deterioration in fundamental rights.[15] They also noted that approximately 69% of the global population experienced the deterioration of the rule of law and that the worst recession occurred during the COVID-19 pandemic.[16] People are living with the crises that result from human activities on earth. What is the ideal legal system necessary to protect the fundamental human rights of every person in the current situation?

In this context, this book focuses on a justice system in a fragile state. The major target of this book is small island developing states (SIDS), which are frequently mentioned in the context of the Anthropocene and global crises such as climate change, due to their vulnerability on the basis of their geographical characteristics. The vulnerability of SIDS under the unequal impact of the global crisis has made them increasingly fragile. While the concepts of development and the Anthropocene are very Westernized and were introduced by developed countries, SIDS have taken a different trajectory from those of continental and large nations. What efforts can be made to protect the fundamental human rights of vulnerable people living in these fragile societies? Specifically, how are the situations and challenges of the fundamental human rights of people in SIDS evaluated from the perspective of "law and development"? Moreover, what are the characteristics of the law and justice model of SIDS in the Anthropocene?

1.2 Aims of the Book: How Should People Ensure the Rule of Law in SIDS?

This book aims to identify the challenges and features of law and development faced by SIDS in the Anthropocene. In this context, this book explores the situation of law and justice in Niue as a case study. The principal research question to be addressed is "What kind of governance and policy initiatives are needed to ensure the rule of law and guarantee people's fundamental human rights in a vulnerable country with a small population?"

Niue is one of the smallest states in the world, with approximately only 1,700 people. It has been a self-governing state in free association with New Zealand since 1974 and is recognized as a small island developing state by the United Nations. In the context of law and justice in Niue, a lack of support for the judiciary exists. Thus, maintaining an appropriate legal system that meets international standards is difficult. Since Niue

15 *supra* note 10, p. 133.
16 *supra* note 10, pp. 130–131.

does not have any libraries or have only limited higher education institutions, such as universities, the country does not have proper archives of law, legal history, or other relevant sources. This situation critically hinders access to justice and an understanding of legal systems and remedies for all the people of Niue, thereby affecting both local people and elites alike. In addition to these domestic conditions, Niue is exposed to various risks in global society. The various global challenges that have emerged with increasing globalization have had diverse effects on SIDS, including Niue, in the context of their development and progress. In the Anthropocene, these unequal impacts must be considered, addressed, and "prepared for."

Against this background, this book explores the current situation of the rule of law among people in Niue and presents policy implications for enhancing judicial mechanisms and people's rights for the future in Niue and, more broadly, for SIDS.

This book has three principal objectives related to addressing this situation. First, through an analysis of the case of Niue, this book can contribute to a broader understanding of the rule of law situation and judicial challenges in SIDS. This book comprehensively considers the rule of law assistance in SIDS and how global society takes responsibility for enhancing it in this context. Through this process, this book can provide implications for future rule of law assistance and strategies.

Second, this book aims to explore the situation of a nation that is often little known and forgotten. In addition to serving as a systematic source of information on Niue's law and justice system for global society as a whole, this book can share legal information to increase the legal awareness and advantage of the people of Niue. As discussed below, Niue is not a member of the United Nations. Information on the legal system in Niue is limited and generally not well known. At the same time, the law and justice situations are difficult to understand even for the people of Niue inside and outside the country. This publication can be an important source of information about not only the Niue legal system itself but also the risks faced. Exploring the situation of this very vulnerable and unique small island nation from the perspective of "SIDS in a global society" can contribute to understanding the challenges a global society faces.

Finally, the book can lead to the substantial guarantee of the people's right to access justice in Niue by achieving the above objective. Niue faces a lack of judicial capacity and has taken measures to handle the judicial system such as regularly hosting judges from New Zealand. Thus, various people, both domestically and internationally, may be involved in legal issues in Niue, and accurate information is essential. The book, as a significant source of law and justice in Niue, can contribute to this.

1.3 Key Concepts of the Book

This section introduces the key concepts of the book, the features of SIDS in the Pacific region, and their laws and development circumstances. This section also explores why consideration of SIDS has become significant in current global society.

1.3.1 Fragile States in the Anthropocene Context

In the Cambridge dictionary, the word "fragile" is defined as "easily damaged, broken, or harmed."[17] However, no internationally agreed-upon definition of the term "fragile state" has been reached; in fact, the definitions of fragile states are diverse. The Organisation for Economic Cooperation and Development (OECD) Development Assistance Committee (DAC) defines a fragile condition as "when state structures lack the political will and/or capacity to provide the basic functions needed for poverty reduction, development, and to safeguard the security and human rights of their population."[18] Regarding the OECD's definition, Mcloughlin notes that its definition reflects the prevailing characterization of state fragility as the failure of states to perform certain functions to meet citizens' basic needs and expectations.[19] The Asian Development Bank (ADB) defines more causes and social conditions such as "a combination of (i) exposure to risk, and (ii) insufficient coping capacity of the state, system, or community to manage, absorb, or mitigate those risks (i.e., resilience capacity)."[20] Additionally, some organizations define fragile states on the basis of indicators. The World Bank, for example, refers to its ranking of state fragility in the country policy and institutional assessment.[21] The Fund for Peace, which is a US-based non-governmental research institute, issues the Fragile State Index every year, which is based on a mixed approach of quantitative, qualitative, and content analysis data with diverse perspectives, including political, social, and economic indicators, to determine fragile states.[22]

Previous research has indicated that state fragility is a multidimensional phenomenon and a matter of degree, and different levels of fragility

17 David Vale, Stephen Mullaney, and Leo Hartas, *The Cambridge Dictionary* (Cambridge: Cambridge University Press, 1996).

18 OECD, DAC, *The Principles for Good International Engagement in Fragile States and Situations* (Paris: OECD, DAC, 2007), p. 19.

19 Claire McLoughlin and Iffat Idris, *Fragile States: Topic Guide* (2016), GSDRC.

20 Asian Development Bank, *A Conceptual Understanding of Fragility in Asia and the Pacific* (2023).

21 The World Bank, "Classification of Fragile and Conflict-Affected Situations."

22 The Fund for Peace, *Fragile States Index Annual Report 2024 (2024).*

depend on dimensions that may coexist in a society.[23] Naude et al. note important contexts for considering the definition of fragile states. First, the meaning of fragile states is different depending on when it is defined. Most of the definitions of fragile states define fragility after the fact.[24] Naude et al. emphasize the necessity of forward-looking definitions and predictive measures of state fragility.[25] Second, state fragility is a degree-oriented matter and that various levels of fragility exist together in one society.[26] Naude et al. suggest four major classifications of causes for fragile status: conflict, low development status, vulnerability, and non-developmental states.[27]

How can SIDS be classified and understood in this context? SIDS are generally fragile because of their vulnerability caused by their geographical conditions. In light of the four major causes of fragile states suggested by Naude et al., SIDS are categorized as vulnerable states, which is a forward-looking concept that refers to a state's potential to be negatively affected by future changes.[28] Their vulnerabilities have stalled development and may aggravate fragile situations.

In the Anthropocene, there are many references to "small island states" as societies that may be greatly affected by the global crisis. In recent years, the Pacific SIDS have been affected by environmental crises such as sea level rise and natural disasters caused by climate change, as well as economic crises at the global level. Climate change, which has accelerated because of human actions or human factors, has had an "unequal" impact

23 Nematullah Bizhan (ed.), *State Fragility: Case Studies and Comparisons* (London: Routledge, Taylor & Francis Group, 2023), pp. 7–8. Wim A. Naudé, Amelia Paulino, Amelia Santos-Uliafnova, and Mark McGillivray (eds), *Fragile States: Causes, Costs, and Responses* (Oxford: Oxford University Press, 2011), pp. 4–5. Lars Engberg-Pedersen, Louise Andersen, and Finn Stepputat, *Fragile Situations: Current Debates and Central Dilemmas*, DIIS Report, no. 9 (2008), p. 7.

24 Naudé et al. (2011), *Ibid.*, pp. 6–7.

25 *Ibid.*

26 Naudé et al. (2011), *supra* note 23, pp. 6–7. Engberg-Pedersen et al. (2008), *supra* note 23, p. 9; Simon Feeny and Mark McGillivray. "Aid and Growth in Small Island Developing States," *Journal of Development Studies* 46, no. 5 (2010), pp. 897–917.

27 In Naude et al.'s definitions of each category, "conflict" refers to states where conflict exists or is likely to exist, such as revolutionary wars, ethnic conflicts, adverse regime changes, genocide, or political killings; low development status are countries such as LDCs and LLDCs that are not in conflict but are severely underdeveloped due to extreme poverty, lack of infrastructure, lack of education and health services, etc.; "fragile" refers to a state that is vulnerable to external shocks, including natural disasters and economic shocks, such as SIDS, as opposed to a state's level of development; and "non-developed states" are those that have institutional capacity but are politically abandoned to development, specifically those that are dependent on resources and external assistance. Naudé et al. (2011), *supra* note 23, pp. 10–18.

28 Naudé et al. (2011), *supra* note 23, pp. 8–11.

on countries globally. As a result, vulnerable countries, such as SIDS, face high risks that are at odds with their development status. As "sustainable" development has become a global goal, it is imperative to consider what approaches are necessary for vulnerable societies and countries while protecting the global condition as a global responsibility.

On the other hand, in the context of SIDS, another perspective has been proposed: specifically, Stratford et al. note the importance of not using the society, culture, and people of SIDS as tools to discuss and analyse the Anthropocene but rather to focus on "how the values, thoughts, and actions of the islanders themselves reveal the context of the Anthropocene."[29] Vitousek and Chadwick note that Pacific island countries have historically adapted to various global changes and environmental challenges and have evolved their own agricultural and other crops. Thus, they can respond to their impacts in the Anthropocene era.[30] From this perspective considering SIDS, which are in a different position from the development processes that have shaped the Anthropocene, may have implications for the state and way of thinking of global society. Specifically, the context of the Anthropocene is influenced by colonial ideas, including the development process and values of Western nations and inequalities in terms of development and environmental impacts. For many SIDS, especially in the Pacific region which has a long history of colonization, the relationship between the Anthropocene and decolonization needs to be considered.[31]

In summary, the vulnerabilities of SIDS and the fragile situation caused by these existing vulnerabilities need to be considered. Governance systems that support fragile societies must be examined. In light of this situation, consideration of SIDS in achieving a "leave no one behind" situation may lead to a comprehensive approach to achieving global goals.

1.3.2 SIDS as Vulnerable States in Global Society

As discussed above, SIDS are categorized as a distinct group of vulnerable states facing specific social, economic, and environmental vulnerabilities. Historically, people from remote and small islands have lived with their own suffering, which comes from the geographical character

29 Elaine Stratford, Carol Farbotko, Phillipa Watson, Taukiei Kitara, Juno Berthelsen, Maria Chnaraki, Ayano Ginoza, Christopher Cozier, and Julie Edel Hardenberg, "Islands, the Anthropocene, and Decolonisation," *Antipode*, 55, no.4 (2023), pp. 1256–1257.

30 Peter Vitousek and Oliver Chadwick, "Pacific Islands in the Anthropocene," *Elementa: Science of the Anthropocene*, 1 (2023), p. 1.

31 Adelman (2021), *supra* note 6, p. 55. Stratford et al. (2023), *supra* note 29, pp. 1268–1270.

of the place in which they reside. The United Nations recognized the category of SIDS for the first time at the Conference on Environment and Development (UNCED) held in Rio de Janeiro in 1992.[32] Subsequently, the United Nations has classified 57 countries and territories, including 39 UN member states and 18 Associate Members of the United Nations Regional Commissions. Among those, 19 states are in the Pacific region.[33] While small island states tend to develop their own culture, language, and society in an isolated environment, they also face common risks and disadvantages in a range of areas. Additionally, many SIDS are vulnerable to external impacts such as sea level rise due to global warming, and achieving sustainable development is considered difficult because of inherent problems based on geographical conditions such as the diffuse, narrow, discrete, and oceanic nature of their land, as well as remoteness from international markets. These geographical features also have a significant impact on industrial and economic activities in individual nations and regions.

SIDS have long sought global recognition of the unique crises faced by these vulnerable countries. To address these particular vulnerabilities, the outcome document "SIDS Accelerated Modalities of Action Pathway (SAMOA Pathway)" was adopted at the 3rd International Conference on Small Island Developing States held in Samoa in 2014. This indicates the significance of tangible initiatives and of enhancing partnerships for sustainable development in SIDS.[34] The following year, the 2030 Agenda for Sustainable Development, which includes the SDGs, was adopted.[35] The responsibility of global society and its response to vulnerable states such as the least developed countries and SIDS are recognized in the principle of "Leave no one behind," and it was confirmed that concerted efforts are essential to achieve the SDGs. In May 2024, the 4th International Conference on Small Island Developing States was held in Antigua and Barbuda. At the conference, the reality that SIDS are at the forefront of economic insecurity and the global climate change crisis was acknowledged with the adoption of the Antigua and Barbuda Agenda for

32 United Nations, Office of the High Representative for the Least Developed Countries, Landlocked Developing Countries and Small Island Developing States, "About Small Island Developing States."

33 States in the Pacific region, including UN member states and non-sovereign states, that are classified as SIDS are as follows: American Samoa, Cook Islands, Commonwealth of Northern Marianas, Federated States of Micronesia, Fiji, French Polynesia, Guam, Kiribati, Marshall Islands, Nauru, New Caledonia, Niue, Palau, Papua New Guinea, Samoa, Solomon Islands, Tonga, Tuvalu, and Vanuatu. *Ibid.*

34 United Nations General Assembly, *A/RES/69/15. SIDS Accelerated Modalities of Action (SAMOA) Pathway* (December 15, 2014).

35 United Nations General Assembly (2015), *supra* note 12.

SIDS (ABAS) – A Renewed Declaration for Resilient Prosperity, which includes a ten-year action plan to achieve sustainable development.[36] A significant milestone for SIDS was the adoption of the Multidimensional Vulnerability Index (MVI) by the United Nations General Assembly in 2024.[37] In response to a request from ABAS, the United Nations Resolution will lead to a comprehensive understanding of the vulnerabilities and risks faced by SIDS and bring about significant changes in development assistance strategies and global cooperation.

Global society recognized that SIDS face "particular vulnerabilities" on the basis of geographical factors and called for solidarity and the need for a response. However, many donors are concerned that the aid impact in SIDS is less effective than aid in other states.[38] The study by Simon Feeny and Mark McGillivray explains that SIDS face greater absorptive capacity constraints, which means that the impact of aid on growth in SIDS is contingent on the quality of the policies and performance of their institutions.[39] Designing aid projects on the basis of approaches appropriate to the recipient society and considering how aid effectiveness can be improved present challenges for the future.

With respect to Pacific island countries, all 14 sovereign states have gained independence from colonizing sovereign states since the 1960s, and many territories still exist within the region.[40] Since some states have few domestic resources and limited economic activities, international organizations and other countries provide bilateral and multilateral aid to SIDS, and a high percentage of donors are former colonial powers. In fact, the major donors to Pacific island countries are Australia and New Zealand, which have close geographical proximity and historical ties,[41] and both Australia and New Zealand allocate more than 60% of their official development assistance (ODA) budgets to Pacific island countries.[42]

36 United Nations, *The Antigua and Barbuda Agenda for SIDS (ABAS)* (2024).

37 United Nations General Assembly, *A/RES/78/322 Multidimensional Vulnerability Index* (August 14, 2024).

38 Feeny et al. (2010), *supra* note 26, pp. 903–905.

39 *Ibid.*

40 The 14 member states of the Pacific Islands Forum, excluding Australia and New Zealand, are Kiribati, Cook Islands, Samoa, Solomon Islands, Tuvalu, Tonga, Nauru, Niue, Vanuatu, Papua New Guinea, Palau, Fiji, Marshall Islands, and the Federated States of Micronesia. Of these, two countries gained independence successively in the 1960s, six in the 1970s, three in the 1980s, and the most recent, the Republic of Palau, in 1994.

41 Lowy Institute, "Pacific Aid Map."

42 Australian Government, Department of Foreign Affairs and Trade, *Australia's Official Development Assistance Development Budget Summary 2024–25* (2024); New Zealand Foreign Affairs and Trade, *Ministry of Foreign Affairs Report on the International Development Cooperation 2022–23* (2023), pp. 49–50.

However, there is another aspect of this aid relationship. Epeli Hau'ofa, a prominent cultural anthropologist in the Pacific islands region, noted that there is an aspect of "small islands aiding their two big neighbours." In other words, by providing aid to island countries, Australia and New Zealand also benefit economically.[43] Hau'ofa explains that decolonization in the Pacific SIDS means "regional integration," since development towards self-reliance is practically impossible from the perspective of a lack of resources essential for national self-reliance.[44] This is related to the fact that the Pacific islands region has created and been sympathetic to regional integration vision and ideas, such as the Blue Pacific (Figure 1.1).[45]

Figure 1.1 A map of Oceania.

Note: Adobe Stock, "Oceania Map (image ID: 166048057)."

43 Epeli Hau'ofa, *We Are the Ocean: Selected Works* (Honolulu: University of Hawaii Press, 2008), pp. 20–21.

44 *Ibid.*

45 The "Blue Pacific" is a term that was established to describe the region of the Pacific Ocean, its island nations, and their collective interests. It was used by Hon. Tuilaepa Sa'ilele Malielegaoi, prime minister of Samoa, in 2017, and inspired by Epeli Hau'ofa.

1.3.3 Law and Justice Systems in the Context of the Pacific SIDS

What does the rule of law and justice look like in the Pacific region? What are the features of SIDS in terms of the rule of law and law and development, especially on Pacific islands?

In the context of SIDS in the Pacific region, vulnerable social conditions impact the judicial system and the rule of law. Although the situation varies depending on individual countries and regions, the following factors can be identified as major trends.

First, modern legal systems were introduced "from the outside" upon independence in many countries. In other words, domestic laws have been developed with influences from former colonial powers; thus, this phenomenon has been referred to as an "inheritance of the law." However, customs and customary laws based on the traditions and values of each region also continue. This situation has created legal pluralism in the Pacific region.

In the pre-colonial Pacific island countries, unwritten laws, such as customs and customary laws, were important in maintaining order within the community.[46] However, in the decolonization process since the 1960s, all Pacific island countries have enacted codified constitutions, which have been influenced by their former colonial powers, e.g., Samoa, Kiribati, Solomon Islands, Fiji, Nauru, and Tuvalu. Other nations where the UK was the former colonial power have common law systems due to the influence of the British. Recognizing the importance of customary law as a social norm that is inherent in society, some Pacific island countries, such as Papua New Guinea, Solomon Islands, Tuvalu, and Vanuatu have formalized the legal status and validity of customary law in their constitutions after gaining independence or self-government.[47]

Teubner describes the transformation when external rules are transplanted into a domestic society as being a "legal irritant." In other words, these events are not mere transplants of rules but can create new situations by restructuring the connection between the law and the existing society.[48] In the process of decolonization, many Pacific island countries have experienced "legal irritants" and social transformation. New legal systems have been constructed, and the values and ways of being in society have been redefined.

Please see Pacific Islands Forum Secretariat, *Forum Communique: Forty-eighth Pacific Islands Forum* (2017).

46 Jennifer Corrin and Vergil Narokobi, *Introduction to South Pacific Law*. 5th ed. (Cambridge: Intersentia, 2022), pp. 2–3.

47 *Ibid.*

48 Gunther Teubner, "Legal Irritants: Good Faith in British Law or How Unifying Law Ends Up in New Divergences," *Modern Law Review*, 61 (1998), pp. 17–23.

Second, some Pacific island countries have a small jurisdiction, and accessible dispute resolution systems such as courts, legal professionals, and judicial services are limited for the general public. The same situation can be seen in remote island areas in archipelagic countries such as Solomon Islands and Papua New Guinea. Additionally, in many island countries, official courts are located only on islands with capitals or major cities, making physical access difficult.[49] To address this problem, Papua New Guinea and Solomon Islands, for example, have adopted a system called a "Court Circuit," in which judges, judicial experts, or justices of the peace travel to cities and remote islands to adjudicate lower court cases and resolve various law-related issues.[50] This Court Circuit system has long been rooted in common law jurisdictions; thus, this is a situation where the influence of former colonial power remains. Regarding Niue, it is an extremely small country with a small population. Owing to the lack of domestic human resources, the High Court judges in Niue are appointed from the Maori Land Court, while the commissioner and the justices of the peace are roles performed by local people. This mechanism also protects the rights of people in geographically isolated or under-resourced areas to access judicial services and is a means of ensuring the right of access to justice for people in SIDS.

Finally, these countries are vulnerable to external factors such as global crises due to the lack of resources in the judicial field. In this context, people's right to access justice can be significantly affected. For example, this feature had a distinctive impact during the COVID-19 pandemic. SIDS may respond to global crises in different ways than large or continental states do. Chapter 4 introduces the case of Niue in more detail in this context.

1.4 Research Destination: "The Rock of Polynesia" as a Case Study

This book focuses on the rule of law in Niue as a case study. The decision to adopt a case study approach and focus on the experiences of a single country reflects the authors' belief in the importance of examining a specific case to consider the effect on society on the basis of the characteristics of a legal system and the situation of the rule of law there.

Niue is located in the Pacific Ocean (Figure 1.2). Since Niue is the largest raised coral atoll on earth, it is commonly referred to as "the Rock of Polynesia." It is home to approximately 1,700 people and consists of

49 National & Supreme Courts of Papua New Guinea, "Provincial Registries."

50 National & Supreme Courts of Papua New Guinea, "*National Court*;" Solomon Islands Government, "About the Office of the Director of Public Prosecutions."

Figure 1.2 A map of Niue.

Note: Adobe Stock, "Niue Map (image ID: 654269888)."

a single isolated island, with its coral reefs and cliffs, of about 261 square kilometres.[51] The population is mostly Niuean, the majority ethnic group, and people speak Niuean and English, which are both official languages. Because of its geographic isolation, Niue has interacted with external actors and developed its society through a unique process among Oceania countries.[52]

In 1774, Captain James Cook was the first European to attempt to land on Niue but he was blocked by local opposition. In 1846, Christian missionaries from the London Missionary Society subsequently landed on Niue to spread Christianity. Starting with the village of Mutalau,

51 Margaret Pointer, *Niue 1774–1974: 200 Years of Contact and Change* (Hawaii: University of Hawaii Press, 2015), preface.

52 *Ibid*. Corrin and Narokobi (2022), *supra* note 46, p. 2.

they gradually expanded their mission to other villages. At first, there was opposition and resistance from the local people; however, gradually Christianity was accepted.[53]

The former king of Niue, Mataio Tuitoga, promulgated written laws and practices that were followed by his successors until 1901.[54] Niue became a British protectorate in 1901 at the Niuean King Fataaiki's request and was annexed to New Zealand the following year. It became a self-governing state in free association with New Zealand on October 19, 1974, under the Niue Constitution Act of 1974.[55] Thus, New Zealand is responsible for conducting foreign affairs and defence at the request of Niue, in consultation with the Government of Niue.[56]

While Niue has a self-governing status, Niue is not a member state of the United Nations. The status of self-governing in free association allows Niue to become a member of UN specialized agencies and regional organizations, such as the Pacific Islands Forum, and to attend UN conferences and treaty conferences such as the UN Ocean Conference and the Conference of Parties of the United Nations Framework Convention on Climate Change (UNFCCC). However, it has been noted that there is a possibility of falling outside the scope of the UN's investigation and monitoring of the situation of international human rights owing to its non-member status.[57] Owing to Niue's status in global society, information has not been released, and sufficient research has not been conducted, especially regarding the human rights situation. This book

53 S. Percy Smith, "Niue Island, and Its People," *The Journal of the Polynesian Society*, 12, 1(45) (1903), pp. 17–21.

54 Pointer (2015), *supra* note 51, pp. 219–221; Corrin and Narokobi (2022), *supra* note 46, p. 2.

55 Government of Niue, "Constitution of Niue – comment," in *Constitution of Niue and Associated Documents as at 31 December 2019* (Niue, 2019), p.v.; Caroline J. McDonald, "An Exemplary Leader?: New Zealand and Decolonization of the Cook Islands and Niue," *The Journal of Pacific History*, 3 (2020), p. 395; Tony Angelo, Elisabeth Perham, and Yi-Shen Lau, *Niue in New Zealand Legislation*, 52 Victoria University of Wellington Law Review (2021), 245–284.

56 The Niue Constitution Act 1974, s. 6.

57 As Niue is not a full member of the United Nations, in principle, it is not the official subject of a UN human rights investigation. Although not subject to review with respect to the Universal Periodic Review (UPR), Niue's human rights situation may be included when New Zealand reports under the UPR. In addition, except for treaties that Niue has ratified separately, such as the Convention on the Rights of the Child, Niue is not a signatory to many human rights treaties, which would not give rise to reporting obligations. United Nations General Assembly, *A/RES/60/251. Resolution adopted by the General Assembly on 15 March 2006: Human Rights Council* (March 15, 2006); United Nations Human Rights Office of the High Commissioner, "Ratification of 18 International Human Rights Treaties"; Erin Thomas, *Who's Left Out? Human Rights in Non-UN Member States and Territories* (Development Policy Center, May 8, 2018).

explores explicit and implicit issues related to justice and the rule of law in Niue.

Niue has 14 villages; its capital is Alofi. Each village has a council which is comprised of five members elected every three years.[58] The Niue legislative assembly is a unicameral legislative assembly.[59] In Niue, a general election is held every three years. The Niue Assembly consists of 20 members: 14 village representatives and 6 from the common roll.[60] To avoid divisive tendencies, a non-party system is effective to ensure solidarity for the common good in Niue.[61]

Niue is categorized as a SIDS. Niue is extremely vulnerable to external shocks, including economic and environmental factors, and faces challenges common to SIDS due to its geographical features. In addition to these problems, Niue faces unique problems caused by its society. Among these, the most serious is depopulation, which threatens its viability as a nation-state.[62] In 1974, when Niue became a self-governing state, approximately 4,500 people lived there, but this number gradually decreased to approximately 1,700 people in 2024.[63] According to a census by the New Zealand government, 30,867 people of Niuean descent live in New Zealand. That accounts for more than 90% of all Niuean people in global society.[64] There are various factors responsible for this situation of migration to New Zealand, such as the difficult lifestyle due to a lack of resources and limited opportunities for education, industry, and jobs as "push" factors and the free association status with New Zealand as a "pull" factor.[65]

During the field interviews conducted by the author in 2023, local people described Niue as follows: "*Niue is not small but empty.*"[66] This situation became a factor in policy related to a four-day work week.[67]

58 The Village Councils Act 2016, s. 4.

59 Government of Niue, "Government and Political System;" Teresia Teaiwa and Malakai Koloamatangi, "Democracy and Its Prospects in the Pacific," in Michael Powles (ed.), *Pacific Futures* (Canberra: Pandanus, 2006), p. 33.

60 Government of Niue, "Government."

61 John Henderson, "Governance and Constitutional Issues: Reflections on Current Problems and Future Options," in Michael Powles (ed.), *Pacific Futures* (Canberra: Pandanus, 2006), p. 15.

62 Transform Aqorau, "Rethinking Sovereignty in the Pacific," in Michael Powles (ed.), *Pacific Futures* (Canberra: Pandanus, 2006), p. 222.

63 Government of Niue, Official Website.

64 New Zealand Foreign Affairs and Trade, "About Niue."

65 Vili Nosa "The Impact of Transnationalism on Niue," in Helen Morton Lee and Steve Tupai Francis (eds), *Migration and Transnationalism: Pacific Perspectives* (Canberra: ANU E Press, 2009), pp. 181–183.

66 Interview with an anonymous interviewee (February 21, 2023) (Alofi, Niue).

67 Thomas (2018), *supra* note 57; Esther Pavihi, "Government to Decide on the Future of the Public Service 4-Day Week," BCN (June 9, 2021).

Niuean people generally work from Monday to Thursday, and the policy encourages people to be engaged in community, church, and other volunteer activities to compensate for the lack of human resources in Niue. Thus, one person often works in various places, and all residents live as multitasking players in Niue.[68]

Another critical issue in Niue is the impact of climate change. The most crucial event was Cyclone Heta in January 2004, which caused extensive damage in Alofi. Cyclone Heta destroyed much of the infrastructure and led to losses of approximately NZ$90 million and two fatalities.[69] Because Cyclone Heta hit the centre of Alofi, where most of the government offices and major facilities were based, the estimated value of the loss was enormous: Niue's only hospital was completely damaged, the Cultural Centre and Museum were destroyed and over 90% of the national collections and archives were lost.[70] On the basis of lessons learned from Cyclone Heta and with funding from the Australian and the New Zealand governments, the Government of Niue decided to relocate the only high school in Niue inland to protect children from natural disasters.[71] Niue Hospital was rebuilt inland, with support from the New Zealand government, the World Health Organization, and the European Union, and a national museum was reconstructed and reopened as the Tāoga Niue Museum in 2018.[72] Niuean society recovered after the event. However, the incident demonstrated the vulnerability of Niue to climate change and extreme natural disasters.

Due to its geographical and environmental background, Niue has a unique social structure. It is necessary for global society to recognize the vulnerability of small island states such as Niue and to consider what measures should be taken.

In the context of law and justice, New Zealand conducts some practical work on its behalf to supplement the small judicial capacity of Niue. The current law of Niue is *Niue Legislation 2019*, which was printed on December 31, 2019, and was influenced by the Niuean society.[73] Niue's legislative and administrative system follows the principles of common

68 *supra* note 66; additionally, please see Pavihi (2021), *Ibid*.

69 South Pacific Regional Environment Programme, "The Loss and Damage of Niue's History," SPREP (July 18, 2023); United Nations, OCHA Relief Web, "Cyclone Heta Hits Tiny Pacific Island of Niue," (January 6, 2004).

70 Jon Barnett and Heidi Ellemor, "'Niue after Cyclone Heta," *The Australian Journal of Emergency Management*, 22, no. 1 (2007).

71 United Nations, OCHA Relief Web, "Protecting Niue's Schoolchildren" (December 11, 2012).

72 South Pacific Regional Environment Programme, *supra* note 69. Barnett and Ellemor (2007), *supra* note 70.

73 Government of Niue, *Niue Legislations as at 31 December 2019*.

law and equity. The laws of Niue enacted by the Niue Assembly consist of the Constitution, Acts of the Assembly, Regulations, Niuean custom, and the common law of Niue, in order of priority.[74] The Constitution of Niue, which is the supreme law, consists of the Niue Constitution Act 1974 and the document called the Constitution of Niue which provides the key rules of the Government of Niue and is a schedule of the Niue Constitution Act 1974.[75]

Before 1974, Niue was governed by an Act of the New Zealand Parliament, the Niue Act 1966.[76] Since Niue became a self-governing state in free association with New Zealand on October 19, 1974, full legislative and executive powers have been with the Niue Assembly and Cabinet under the Constitution of Niue.[77] The laws of Niue explicitly include provisions for customs, which determine the rights of customary land.

The law of Niue and its legislative process are decolonized and independent. The amendment of laws in New Zealand no longer affects the laws of Niue and vice versa.[78] While New Zealand may provide technical assistance at Niue's request in drafting and ensuring the rule of law, Niue is responsible for the final decision, including whether the draft and legal systems fit Niuean society. However, some components of Niue laws are similar to the laws of New Zealand as pre-1974 laws were made by the New Zealand parliament and many of those laws continue to be in force, although such legislation may not be coincident with the actual Niue law.[79] Niue's judicial system is separate from that of New Zealand. Thus, legal practitioners must appreciate not only the laws themselves but also the relationship and complexity of the legislation of Niue and New Zealand. Angelo et al. noted that the two legal systems have developed independently.[80] Insofar as New Zealand judges and lawyers may be involved, knowledge of Niue law should be essential.

In the context of the decolonization process in law and justice, a significant milestone in the history of Niue occurred in August 2024. On October 19, 2024, Niue celebrated its 50th anniversary of gaining self-governing status, and an official ceremony was held at the Hanan International Airport in Niue on Constitution Day. Prior to the 50th anniversary celebration, Niue held a referendum to consider four proposed

74 The Interpretation Act 2004, s. 4.
75 Government of Niue (2019), *supra* note 55, p. v.
76 Government of Niue, *supra* note 59.
77 Constitution of Niue, Art. 28 (3); Angelo, Perham, and Lau (2021), *supra* note 55, pp. 246–247.
78 Angelo, Perham, and Lau (2021), *supra* note 55, pp. 246–247.
79 *Ibid.*
80 Angelo, Perham, and Lau (2021), *supra* note 55, p. 247.

amendments to the 1974 Constitution. This was a historic event, as it was only the second referendum since Niue became a self-governing state in 1974.[81] The proposed 2024 Niue Constitution Amendment Bills included four proposals: 1) to change the title from "Premier" to "Prime Minister"; 2) to increase the total number of Cabinet Ministers from four to six; 3) to extend the term of the Niue Assembly from three to four years; and 4) to amend the reference in the Constitution from the Audit Office to Auditor-General.[82] In accordance with Article 35 of the Constitution of Niue, a referendum was held on August 31, 2024. As a result, issues 1) and 4) were approved (issue 1 partially); issues 2) and 3) were rejected.[83] The four Constitutional Amendment Bills of 2024 revealed a move towards a more mature and independent governance system. In other words, Niue aimed to strengthen independence and self-governance and to shift to a system more adapted to global society. However, of the four issues for a constitutional amendment, both rejected issues 2) and 3) are related to the expansion of the size of Cabinet and the extension of the term of the Assembly. These results reveal the cautious attitude of the people of Niue towards change and Cabinet expansion.

Thus, Niue has been seeking, hesitatingly, and progressing as a nation-state in the 50 years since gaining self-governing status in 1974. Her progress has, in the changing times of the Anthropocene, wavered in the process of decolonization, self-reliance, and development.

1.5 An Overview of the Book

This book consists of six chapters that explore the law and justice systems of Niue as a small island developing state. The introductory chapter overviews the objectives of the book, the research methodology, the principal research question, and the overall structure of the book. Chapter 1 introduces key concepts and their frameworks that analyse the

81 The first constitutional amendment since 1974 was implemented on June 13, 1992, under Article 35 of the Niue Constitution. The amendment bills in 1992 included: 1) the introduction of the Niue High Court and Court of Appeal in Niue; 2) the abolition of the Niue Land Court and the Land Court of Appeal and the establishment of a Land Division in the High Court; 3) the requirement for Niue politicians to retain their New Zealand citizenship; and 4) the removal of Article 31 of the constitution (special provisions for measures affecting criminal law or personal character). At the referendum, 70.4% of the valid votes (86% of the votes cast) were cast in favour of these proposed amendments, the amendments were passed and the revised constitution went into effect on July 1, 1992. United Nations Economic and Social Council, *E/1990/5/Add.12 Implementation of the International Covenant on Economic, Social and Cultural Rights* (September 23, 1992).

82 Government of Niue, "Official Results of the Niue Constitutional Amendment Referendum," (September 3, 2024).

83 *Ibid.*

situation of law and justice in the context of SIDS. This chapter also explains the background and brief information about Niue and the reason for choosing Niue as a research destination.

Chapter 2 delves into the case of Niue and its society. This chapter provides general information about Niue. It contains references to the history, traditions, culture, people, and social structure of Niue to clarify how the current Niuean society has been formed. This chapter also highlights the challenges that are currently faced by the people.

Chapter 3, Law and Justice in Niue, focuses on the historical context surrounding the development of law and the judicial systems of Niue. This chapter addresses what legal pluralism is for Niue. This leads to a discussion of what that means for the people and the challenges in the context of the rule of law.

Chapter 4 considers the effect of the tangible impact of global society on Niue's judicial systems. Specifically, the chapter analyses the pre- and post-COVID-19 pandemic situation of access to justice in Niue. Given the unique and vulnerable capacity of the justice system, Chapter 4 examines how the impact of the global pandemic transformed existing issues in the justice sector and access to justice for people in Niue. It also analyses the significant social consequences of the pandemic as a global crisis and considers the potential negative effects and fragile features of justice in small island states.

Chapter 5 returns to the principal research question of the book and attempts to answer it by identifying the situation of law and justice and current challenges in Niue. This chapter recaps the key concepts and theoretical framework of law and development introduced in Chapter 1 and reconsiders the paradigm and practices required to enhance the rule of law in the Anthropocene. Additionally, this chapter explores experiences with rule of law assistance in the Pacific SIDS and analyses Niue from a comparative perspective. Since the SIDS in the Pacific region have been seriously affected by climate change and other crises, a global society must consider how we should fulfil our responsibility to ensure the human rights of people in vulnerable societies. This chapter also identifies the remarkable features of SIDS in the context of law on the basis of Niue narratives and aims to lead suggestions for the rule of law assistance and the role of a global society.

Chapter 6 concludes the book with a summary of Niue's law and justice context, its unique challenges and suggestions for legal reform, policy adjustments and future implementation plans in the judicial sector.

The title of the book, *Law and Justice in Small Island Developing States: Lessons from Niue*, has a subtitle, *Tutonuhia he tagata Niue*, that means "the rights and interests of a Niuean person" in Vagahau Niue (the Niuean language). This indicates respect for the laws and institutions that guarantee the human rights of the people and Niuean society and of small island states more broadly.

This book was written by two authors with the same interests and aspirations for law and justice but from very different backgrounds and positions: Mana Takahashi, an academic scholar from Japan (outside of Niue), and Kahealani Sinahemana Hekau, a legal practitioner and politician from Niue (inside of Niue). The authors hope that readers will explore not only Niue and the Pacific SIDS but also the views expressed in this book, which are the result of a chemical interaction between these different perspectives.

References

Literature

Adelman, Sam, "Beyond Development: Towards Sustainability and Climate Justice in the Anthropocene," in Sam Adelman and Abdul Paliwala (eds.), *The Limits of Law and Development* (New York: Routledge, 2021).

Adobe Stock, "Niue Map (image ID: 654269888)." available at: <https://stock.adobe.com/>, accessed August 25, 2025.

Adobe Stock, "Oceania Map (image ID: 166048057)." available at: <https://stock.adobe.com/>, accessed August 25, 2025.

Angelo, Tony, Elisabeth Perham, and Yi-Shen Lau, "Niue in New Zealand Legislation," *Victoria University of Wellington Law Review,* 52 (2021), 245–284.

Aqorau, Transform, "Rethinking Sovereignty in the Pacific," in Michael Powles (eds.), *Pacific Futures* (Canberra, ACT: Pandanus, 2006).

Asian Development Bank, *A Conceptual Understanding of Fragility in Asia and the Pacific* (2023), available at: <https://www.adb.org/sites/default/files/publication/920606/conceptual-understanding-fragility-asia-pacific.pdf>.

Australian Government, Department of Foreign Affairs and Trade, *Australia's Official Development Assistance Development Budget Summary 2024–25* (2024), available at: <https://www.dfat.gov.au/sites/default/files/oda-development-budget-summary-2024-25.pdf>.

Barnett, Jon and Heidi Ellemor, "Niue after Cyclone Heta," *The Australian Journal of Emergency Management,* 22, no. 1 (2007), 3–4.

Bizhan, Nematullah (ed.), *State Fragility: Case Studies and Comparisons* (London: Routledge, Taylor & Francis Group, 2023).

Corrin, Jennifer, and Vergil Narokobi, *Introduction to South Pacific Law* (5th ed. Cambridge: Intersentia, 2022).

Engberg-Pedersen, Lars, Louise Andersen, and Finn Stepputat, *Fragile Situations: Current Debates and Central Dilemmas,* DIIS Report, no. 9 (2008).

Feeny, Simon, and Mark McGillivray, "Aid and Growth in Small Island Developing States," *Journal of Development Studies,* 46, no. 5 (2010), 897–917.

The Fund for Peace, *Fragile States Index Annual Report 2024 (2024),* available at: <https://fragilestatesindex.org/wp-content/uploads/2025/02/FSI-2024-Report-A-World-Adrift-2.pdf>.

Government of Niue, Official Website, available at: <https://www.gov.nu/>, accessed July 27, 2025.

Government of Niue, "Constitution of Niue – Comment," in *Constitution of Niue and Associated Documents as at 31 December 2019* (Niue, 2019).

Government of Niue, "Government and Political System." available at: <https://www.gov.nu/government#political-system/>, accessed July 27, 2025.

Government of Niue, "Government." available at: <https://www.gov.nu/government/>, accessed July 27, 2025.

Government of Niue, "Official Results of the Niue Constitutional Amendment Referendum," (September 3, 2024), available at: <https://www.gov.nu/media-releases/official-results-of-the-niue-constitutional-amendment-referendum>, accessed July 27, 2025.

Government of Niue, "Official Website of COVID-19 Information for Niue: Travel to Niue." available at: <https://covid19.gov.nu/index.php/resources/>, accessed January 6, 2024.

Government of Niue, *Niue Legislation as at 31 December 2019.* available at: <https://www.gov.nu/wp-content/uploads/2022/03/niue_laws_vol1_i12022.pdf>.

Hau'ofa, Epeli, *We Are the Ocean: Selected Works* (Honolulu: University of Hawaii Press, 2008).

Henderson, John, "Governance and Constitutional Issues: Reflections on Current Problems and Future Options," in Michael Powles (eds.), *Pacific Futures* (Canberra, ACT: Pandanus, 2006).

Lowy Institute, "Pacific Aid Map." available at: <https://pacificaidmap.lowyinstitute.org/>, accessed July 27, 2025.

McDonald, Caroline J., "An Exemplary Leader?: New Zealand and Decolonization of the Cook Islands and Niue," *The Journal of Pacific History*, 3 (2020), 394–417.

Mcloughlin, Claire, and Iffat Idris, *Fragile States: Topic Guide* (2016), GSDRC. available at: <https://gsdrc.org/wp-content/uploads/2016/03/FragileStates.pdf>.

Montoya, Maria, and Alejandro Ponce, "Rule-of-Law Backsliding: Where, How, and Why," in Gregory Shaffer and Wayne Sandholtz (eds.), *The Rule of Law Under Pressure: A Transnational Challenge* (New York: Cambridge University Press, 2025).

National & Supreme Courts of Papua New Guinea, "Provincial Registries." available at: <https://www.pngjudiciary.gov.pg/national-court/provincial-registries>, accessed July 27, 2025.

National & Supreme Courts of Papua New Guinea, "National Court." available at: <https://www.pngjudiciary.gov.pg/index.php/national-court>, accessed July 27, 2025.

Naudé, Wim A., Amelia Paulino Amelia Santos-Uliafnova, and Mark McGillivray (eds.), *Fragile States: Causes, Costs, and Responses* (Oxford: Oxford University Press, 2011).

Newton Cain, Tess, "The Incorporation of Customary Law & Principle into Sentencing Decisions in the South Pacific Region," in Anita Jowitt and Tess Newton Cain (eds.), *Passage of Change: Law, Society and Governance in the Pacific* (Canberra: Pandanus Books, 2003).

New Zealand Foreign Affairs and Trade, "About Niue." available at: <https://www.mfat.govt.nz/en/countries-and-regions/australia-and-pacific/niue/new-zealand-high-commission-to-niue/about-niue/>, accessed January 6, 2024.

New Zealand Foreign Affairs and Trade, *Ministry of Foreign Affairs Report on the International Development Cooperation 2022–23* (2023), available at: <https://www.mfat.govt.nz/assets/Aid-Prog-docs/Policy/Minister-of-Foreign-Affairs-report-on-the-International-Development-Cooperation-2022-23.pdf>.

Nosa, Vili, "The Impact of Transnationalism on Niue," in Helen Morton Lee and Steve Tupai Francis (eds.), *Migration and Transnationalism: Pacific Perspectives* (Canberra, ACT: ANU E Press, 2009).

OECD, DAC, *The Principles for Good International Engagement in Fragile States and Situations* (Paris: OECD, DAC, 2007).

Pacific Islands Forum Secretariat, *Forum Communique: Forty-eighth Pacific Islands Forum* (2017), available at: <https://www.forumsec.org/wp-content/uploads/2018/02/Final_48-PIF-Communique_2017_14Sep17.pdf.>.

Pavihi, Esther, "Government to Decide on the Future of the Public Service 4-Day Week." BCN (June 9, 2021), available at: <https://tvniue.com/2021/06/government-to-decide-on-the-future-of-the-public-service-4-day-week/>, accessed July 27, 2025.

Pointer, Margaret, *Niue 1774–1974: 200 Years of Contact and Change* (Otago: Otago University Press, 2015).

Schimmelfennig, Frank, "A Comparison of the Rule of Law Promotion Policies of Major Western Powers," in Michael Zürn, André Nolkaemper, and Randall Peerenboom (eds.), *Rule of Law Dynamics* (New York: Cambridge University Press, 2012).

Shigihara, Atsuko and Nanako Shimizu, "Hitoshinsei no Heiwagaku (in Japanese)," *Heiwa Kenkyu*, 58 (2023), i-viii.

Smith, S. Percy, "Niue Island, and Its People," *The Journal of the Polynesian Society*, 12, no. 1(45) (1903), 1–21.

Solomon Islands Government, "About the Office of the Director of Public Prosecutions." available at: <https://solomons.gov.sb/ministry-of-justice-and-legal-affairs/office-of-the-director-of-public-prosecutions/>, accessed July 27, 2025.

South Pacific Regional Environment Programme, "The Loss and Damage of Niue's History." SPREP (July 18, 2023), available at: <https://www.sprep.org/news/the-loss-and-damage-of-niues-history>, accessed July 27, 2025.

Stratford, Elaine, Carol Farbotko, Phillipa Watson, Taukiei Kitara, Juno Berthelsen, Maria Chnaraki, Ayano Ginoza, Christopher Cozier, and Julie Edel Hardenberg, "Islands, the Anthropocene, and Decolonisation," *Antipode*, 55, no. 4 (2023), 1255–1274.

Teaiwa, Teresia and Malakai Koloamatangi, "Democracy and Its Prospects in the Pacific," in Michael Powles (eds.), *Pacific Futures* (Canberra, ACT: Pandanus, 2006).

Teubner, Gunther, "Legal Irritants: Good Faith in British Law or How Unifying Law Ends Up in New Divergences," *Modern Law Review*, 61 (1998), 11–32.

Thomas, Erin, *Assessing Gender-based Violence in Niue* (ICAAD, 2017), available at: <https://icaad.ngo/wp-content/uploads/2017/11/Assessing-Gender-based-Violence-in-Niue.pdf>.

Thomas, Erin, *Who's Left Out? Human Rights in Non-UN Member States and Territories* (Development Policy center, May 8, 2018), available at: <https://devpolicy.org/human-rights-non-un-member-states-and-territories-20180508/>, accessed July 27, 2025.

UNDP, *New Threats to Human Security in the Anthropocene* (2022), available at: <https://hs.hdr.undp.org/pdf/srhs2022.pdf>.

UNDP, "Human Development Index (HDI)." available at: <https://hdr.undp.org/data-center/human-development-index#/indicies/HD>, accessed July 27, 2025.

United Nations General Assembly, *A/RES/60/251. Resolution Adopted by the General Assembly on 15 March 2006: Human Rights Council* (March 15, 2006).

United Nations General Assembly, *A/RES/69/15. SIDS Accelerated Modalities of Action (SAMOA) Pathway* (December 15, 2014).

United Nations General Assembly, *A/RES/70/1 Transforming Our World: The 2030 Agenda for Sustainable Development* (October 21, 2015).

United Nations General Assembly, *A/RES/78/322 Multidimensional Vulnerability Index* (August 14, 2024).

United Nations and the Rule of Law, "What Is the Rule of Law." available at: <https://www.un.org/ruleoflaw/what-is-the-rule-of-law/>, accessed July 27, 2025.

United Nations Economic and Social Council, *E/1990/5/Add.12 Implementation of the International Covenant on Economic, Social and Cultural Rights* (September 23, 1992).

United Nations, Office of the High Representative for the Least Developed Countries, Landlocked Developing Countries and Small Island Developing States, "About Small Island Developing States." available at: <https://www.un.org/ohrlls/content/about-small-island-developing-states>, accessed July 27, 2025.

United Nations, *The Antigua and Barbuda Agenda for SIDS (ABAS)* (2024), available at: <https://sdgs.un.org/sites/default/files/2024-04/SIDS4%20-%20Co-Chairs%20FINAL.pdf>.

United Nations, *COVID-19 and Human Rights: We Are All in This Together* (2020), available at: <https://unsdg.un.org/sites/default/files/2020-04/COVID-19-and-Human-Rights.pdf>.

United Nations, OCHA Relief Web, "Cyclone Heta Hits Tiny Pacific Island of Niue." (6 January, 2004), available at: <https://reliefweb.int/report/niue-new-zealand/cyclone-heta-hits-tiny-pacific-island-niue>, accessed July 27, 2025.

United Nations, OCHA Relief Web, "Protecting Niue's School Children." (December 11, 2012), available at: <https://reliefweb.int/report/niue-new-zealand/protecting-niue%E2%80%99s-school-children>, accessed July 27, 2025.

United Nations Human Rights Office of the High Commissioner, "Ratification of 18 International Human Rights Treaties." available at: <https://indicators.ohchr.org/>, accessed July 27, 2025.

Vale, David, Stephen Mullaney, and Leo Hartas, *The Cambridge Dictionary* (Cambridge: Cambridge University Press, 1996).
Vitousek, Peter, and Oliver Chadwick, "Pacific Islands in the Anthropocene," *Elementa: Science of the Anthropocene*, 1 (2023), 1–4.
The World Bank, "Classification of Fragile and Conflict-Affected Situations." available at: <https://www.worldbank.org/en/topic/fragilityconflictviolence/brief/classification-of-fragile-and-conflict-affected-situations>, accessed July 27, 2025.
World Justice Project, "What Is the Rule of Law." available at: <https://worldjusticeproject.org/about-us/overview/what-rule-law>, accessed July 27, 2025.
Zürn, Michael, André Nolkaemper, and Randall Peerenboom, "Rule of Law Dynamics in an Era of International and Transnational Governance," in Michael Zürn, André Nolkaemper, and Randall Peerenboom (eds.), *Rule of Law Dynamics* (New York: Cambridge University Press, 2012).

Interviews

Interview with an anonymous interviewee. (February 21, 2023) (Alofi, Niue).

Legislation

Constitution of Niue (2019).
Interpretation Act (2004).
Niue Constitution Act (1974).
Niue Amendment Act (No. 2) (1968).
Village Councils Act (2016).

2 Case Study

A Narrative of Niue

Kahealani Sinahemana Hekau

2.1 General Information on Niue

Niue, known as the Rock of Polynesia, is a small island developing state (SIDS) among several of the Polynesian islands in the South Pacific. It is a self-governing state in free association with New Zealand.[1] It is a part of the Realm of New Zealand.[2] On October 19, 1974, Niue decolonized from New Zealand and established by constitution its three branches of government, namely the Executive, Legislature, and Judiciary. The Executive consists of a prime minister and three cabinet ministers. The Legislature (The Niue Assembly) consists of a speaker and 20 elected representatives made up of a representative each from the 14 villages, and 6 representatives on the common roll with a representative role on behalf of the whole island. The Judiciary is composed of a Court of Appeal presided over by the chief justice and the High Court. At the High Court, criminal division, the lower level is presided over by a commissioner and two justices of the peace. At the High Court, land division, at least three land commissioners preside at the lower level. Appeals from law commissioners at the lower court are heard before a judge of the High Court.

On the world map, Niue is located at latitude −19° 03′ 28.80″ S and longitude −169° 52′ 6.59″ W[3] between the Polynesian triangle comprising the Cook Islands to the east, Tonga to the south, and Samoa to the north. It is 1081.48 kilometres from the Cook Islands to the East,[4] 603.504 kilometres from Tonga to the South,[5] and 632.472 kilometres from Samoa to the North.[6] It is a single island made up of raised coral. It is about 261 square kilometres with the highest point being 68 m above

1 Niue Constitution Act 1974, Government of Niue.

2 Letters Patent Constituting the Office of the Governor-General of New Zealand 1983/225, Clause 1.

3 Satellite map of Niue.

4 Geodatos.net, "Distance from Cook Islands to Niue."

5 Geodatos.net, "Distance from Tonga to Niue."

6 Geodatos.net, "Distance from Niue to Samoa."

DOI: 10.4324/9781003585688-2

sea level.[7] "It has a fringing reef quite close to the shore (…). Intersecting this reef in numerous places are narrow and often deep chasms."[8]

Physically, the island is rugged and appears to have at least two terraces. The lower terrace is along the leeward side, also referred to as the west coast. The upper terrace is characterized by tall cliffs and chasms, with villages that are located further inland. It has a gradual descent to the coastline, unlike the lower terrace, which has a dramatic shoreline, with some villages having open ocean views. There are advantages and disadvantages to both settings.

As of 2022, Niue's resident population of just under 1,700 people – by life stage comprised 26.2% children under the age of 14, 22.3% of those 60 or above, and the remaining working age group from 16 to 59 years of age makes up the balance of 51.5%.[9] Niue has a high-dependency population almost equal to that of the working age group. "Niue's dependency ratio calculates at 94 dependents per 100 people of working age."[10] In the five-year period 1987–1991, the life expectancy for males was 71.1 and for females 76.2.[11] There was minimal change in later years during the five-year period of 2012–2016, where the life expectancy for males was 71.8 and for females 75.7.[12] Among the challenges experienced by the people is a high prevalence of non-communicable diseases. In 2013, "Over one-third of the population was hypertensive, 42.1% of men and 34.9% of women had raised blood glucose, and 34.8% of the population had raised total cholesterol levels. More than 60% of the population were obese."[13] The Department of Health urged the prioritization of "primary and secondary prevention activities."[14] All residents have access to universal healthcare at the local Niue Foou Hospital. Patients with serious conditions are referred for specialist care in New Zealand.

The island is divided into 14 villages: Alofi North, Makefu, Tuapa, Namukulu, Hikutavake, Toi, Mutalau, Lakepa, Liku, Hakupu, Vaiea, Avatele, Tamakautoga, and Alofi South. The west coast villages – Hikutavake to Avatele – are exposed due to their location that faces the direction of oncoming cyclones during the cyclone season. The traditional

7 South Pacific Community, "Niue."

8 S. Percy Smith, *Niue: The Island and Its People, Institute of Pacific Studies* (Suva: University of the South Pacific, 1983).

9 Niue Census of Population and Housing, 2022.

10 Government of Niue, Statistics and Immigration Office, Ministry of Finance and Planning "Statistical Release: Niue Census of Population and Housing, Preliminary Report" (2022).

11 Government of Niue, Ministry of Finance and Planning, "Health Indicators 1987–1991."

12 Government of Niue, Ministry of Finance and Planning, "Health Indicators 2012–2016."

13 Niue Health Department and World Health Organization, *NCD Risk Factors Steps Report* (2013), p. 7.

14 *Ibid.*, p. 10.

boundaries between villages differ somewhat from the boundaries of the 14 constituencies for the election of members to the Niue Assembly.[15] Each of the villages is connected by a circular island public road, vehicle tracks, and foot tracks.[16] Village life is regulated by the local government known as the village council and consists of five members elected every three years. Its functions include the maintenance of the council roads, sea tracks, fishing grounds, health and sanitation of dwellings, prevention of infectious diseases, prevention and abatement of nuisances, regulation of markets and commercial enterprises, and the maintenance of the peace and security of its residents, among other things.[17] A council may, with the approval of cabinet, enact by-laws for the performance of any of its functions.[18]

Niue vegetation is typical of that found in Polynesia. Several studies of Niue vegetation were made over the years, by Yuncker in 1943,[19] Sykes in 1970,[20] Whistler in 1984[21] and 2013,[22] and by Gardner in 2011.[23] Whistler observed that prior to Polynesian settlement, "most of Niue was covered in dense tropical forest."[24] Extensive forest cover spans at least 70% of the land area.[25] After human habitation and exposure to cyclones, the vegetation consists of mature forest, secondary forest, and scrub or barren areas. Knowledge of Niue's vegetation is necessary to understand customary law in relation to Niuean land. Niuean land is the only area where Niuean custom is formally recognized as a source of law. Niuean custom relies on the presence of trees and vegetation as important boundary markers or sanctuaries for coconut crab and birds, which provide important evidence of the use and care of the land by the landowners.

Niue's territorial waters include territorial sea baselines "measured seaward from the baseline, every point at which is distant by 12 nautical miles from the nearest point of the baseline on the low water mark along the coast of Niue, or where there is coral reef along any part of the coast of Niue, the low water mark along the outer edge of the Reef."[26] The exclusive economic zone (EEZ) comprising the sea, seabed and subsoil

15 Niue Assembly Act 1966, Government of Niue, s. 5.
16 Warrant declaring land to be roads, Government of Niue (1971).
17 Village Councils Act 2016, s. 18.
18 *supra* note 17, s. 21.
19 G.G. Yuncker, *The Flora of Niue Island* (B.P. Bishop Museum Bull., 1943).
20 W.R. Sykes, *Contributions to the Flora of Niue* (N.Z. Department of Science and Industrial Research Bull., 1970).
21 W.A. Whistler, *Notes on the Flora of Niue* (N.Z Journal of Botany, 1984).
22 W.A. Whistler, *The Rare Plants of Niue* (Honolulu: Isle Botanica, 2013).
23 R.O. Gardner, *Trees and Shrubs of Niue* (Auckland: Katsura, 2011).
24 *supra* note 22, p. 9.
25 National Biodiversity Strategy and Action Plan (2015), p. 7.
26 Maritime Zones Act (2013), s. 3 and 4.

beyond and adjacent to the territorial sea is measured at 200 nautical miles outward from the nearest point of the baseline.[27] In 2020 Niue declared 40% of its EEZ a marine protected area known as the Niue Moana Mahu Marine Protected Area that is free from extractive activities but supports other reasonable ecologically sustainable use.[28] At the same time, a special management area known as the Beveridge Reef Nukutulueatama Special Management Area was declared for the purpose of preserving and protecting "Beveridge Reef as an outstanding ecological jewel in Niue's ocean."[29] It is not known whether these mechanisms adequately incorporate the inherent conservation customary practices that precede them.

Access to land and safe landing from the sea is by way of the wharf located in Alofi at the boundary line between Alofi South and Alofi North. When the regular supply ship calls, it anchors at the outer edge of the reef. Cargo containers are lifted onto a barge which carries them to the wharf where they are subsequently lifted to the surface of the wharf by crane. There is a monthly shipping service providing supplies to the island. An airport is located in Alofi South and services flights twice a week between Niue and Auckland by Air New Zealand. The peak tourist travel season is April until November. During December to March, the travellers are predominantly visiting family and friends.

Niue's calendar and standard time are one day behind the calendar in New Zealand, and the standard time is the solar time of longitude 165 degrees west of Greenwich.[30]

The average surface temperature is 24 degrees Celsius with minimal change between seasons.[31] There are two seasons in the year, that is, the hot and wet season from November to March with temperatures as high as 30 degrees Celsius, and the cool and dry season from April to November with temperatures averaging 26 degrees Celsius. The hot and wet season is also the cyclone season.[32] The island experiences high humidity during the hot season but longer sunshine hours. The cool and dry season is pleasant but the days have shorter sunshine hours. Over a 40-year period, at least 10 cyclones per decade crossed Niue's EEZ. Between 1981 and 2010, 6 out of 24 tropical cyclones became severe events.[33] In 2004, Niue experienced a category 5 cyclone which caused

27 *supra* note 26, s. 9.
28 Niue Moana Mahu Marine Protected Area Regulations (2020), s. 4(3).
29 *supra* note 28, s. 5(3).
30 Interpretation Act (2004), s. 29.
31 Pacific – Australia Climate Change Science and Adaptation Planning Program. "Current and Future Climate of Niue," p. 2.
32 Government of Niue, "Niue Island Initial National Communication, United Nations Framework Convention on Climate Change" (2000).
33 *Ibid.*

widespread damage. Living through cyclones has had a strong influence on the way of life ranging from relocation of homes, migration, and review of the building code.

The official languages of the Assembly are English and Niuean.[34] The people of Niue preserve their oral history through song, dance, arts, and crafts. Songs and dances are integral to maintaining identity, uniting the community and creating entertainment and joy. Niuean arts and crafts are unique due to their intricate nature and rarity. The law for the promotion and preservation of Niuean custom, protection of traditional knowledge, and expressions of culture was promulgated in 2012.[35]

Niue's communications and internet connectivity are delivered by a 4G fibre network via Telecom Niue Limited. The service was fast and efficient, at least until June 2025 when Alofi and certain locations exceeded the network's capacity due to an unprecedented speed of growth.[36]

2.2 Niue History and Traditions

Several attempts have been made to record the history of Niue over various periods. The early records of Niue history were by S. Percy Smith (1902)[37] and Edwin M. Loeb (1924).[38] The first compilation of Niue history made by 12 Niuean authors was in 1982.[39] A recent work by Margaret Pointer (2015) is also very useful.[40] The statements in this chapter will predominantly rely on the works by the twelve Niuean authors with reference to other works as appropriate.

According to local history, at around 1500 AD, the first inhabitants of Niue were Huanaki and Fao, who came from Tavaii, Fonuagalo (Fonua = land, galo = lost; therefore, the unknown land) or Lalofonua (Lalo = below, fonua = land; therefore, land beneath). They were later joined by Lageiki, Lagiatea, and Talimainuku (Fakahoko).[41] Soon after, these men were revered no longer as men but as gods. This was derived from

34 Constitution of Niue (2019), Art. 23.

35 Taoga Niue Act (2012).

36 Interview with CEO of Telecom Niue Limited, June 2025.

37 *supra* note 8.

38 Edwin M. Loeb. *History and Traditions of Niue* (Honolulu: Bernice P. Bishop Museum, Bulletin 32, 1926).

39 Terry Chapman et al., *Niue: A History of the Island* (Suva: University of the South Pacific and the Government of Niue,1982).

40 Margaret Pointer, *Niue 1774–1974, 200 Years of Contact and Change* (Otago: Otago University Press, 2015).

41 Vilisoni Kumitau and Maihetoe Hekau, "Ko e Tupuaga he tau Tagata Niue" in Terry Chapman et al., *Niue: A History of the Island* (Suva: University of the South Pacific and the Government of Niue,1982), p. 2.

a belief that only gods possessed the superhuman powers responsible for the building up of Niue.[42]

Indeed, the far-flung and isolated location of the island and its rugged terrain would have meant that its first inhabitants came from a line of hard-working men and women. This observation was made later by Smith in 1901, where he stated, "In industry, I think the Niue people compare very favourably with any other branch of the race I met. They are hard workers; indeed, the nature of their island obliges them to work in order to live."[43]

Although there were no ancient places of worship or statues of gods on the island, the people themselves held strong beliefs in their own gods. Their gods were prayed to for rain, for abundance, and for victory during war. For instance, there is the god Leomatagi in the north west whose power is to catch the wind and hide it away in a cave so that the sea is calm and mild. There is the Tokamotu which was an object of worship that was believed to have the power to make rain, or to bring abundance of food and plenty among the people. There is the god Huanaki who had control over the sea, and the main god Tagaloa who was believed to reign over all.[44]

During this period prior to contact with the outside world, settlements began in small and scattered groups close to where there is easy access to land and sea resources. As the island population gradually grew and interaction became frequent, four main settlements came to exist over time: "Paluki between Alofi and Liku, Fatuaua in Tuapa, Falehavaiki in Vaiea and Fetuna between Mutalau and Lakepa."[45]

The descendants of Fao later became kings of Niue during their lifetime.[46] The role of the king was an acquired role – he was elected to the role. He was chosen in recognition of his courage and skill from among a line of warriors.[47] The king carried the responsibility of ensuring the safety of the people and blessings of abundance on the island. If the island experienced some form of natural disaster, for instance when there was a drought, the blame fell on the king. This usually led to his removal.[48] This

42 *supra* note 8.

43 *supra* note 34, art. 35.

44 I. Etuata and P. Tanaki "Tau Atua Tuai he Motu ko Niue he Vaha Pouli," in Terry Chapman et al., *Niue: A History of the Island* (Suva: University of the South Pacific and the Government of Niue,1982), pp. 18–19.

45 *supra* note 40, p. 13.

46 *supra* note 8, p. 4.

47 Hafe Vilitama, "Ko e Fakatufono Motu he Vaha i Tuai i Niue," in Terry Chapman et al., *Niue: A History of the Island* (Suva: University of the South Pacific and the Government of Niue,1982), pp.18–19.

48 *supra* note 40, p. 21.

was attached to the belief that a king had to have had spiritual powers and was expected to be able to control rain. On the other hand, a king could be removed for actual misconduct. A king called Punimata was anointed in Hakupu at the east side who afterwards moved to Tuapa in the north west. He was gifted the Matapa chasm as his bathing place.[49] His reign was peaceful.

The king was assisted by a council comprised of representatives from the rest of the island. This ensured that the king was in touch with the people. Due to the practice that a king could be removed by death if found at fault for not providing blessings for the island, the position of a king sometimes had long vacancies.[50] During such an interregnum, a council of chiefs would rule separately and form laws relating to matters such as tributes of the first fruits and the cooking of food.[51]

The records of Smith and Loeb differ in respect of the origins of kingship on Niue. Smith provides that the nearest reference is from Mangaia in the Cook Islands where a king was chosen, not inherited. It is entirely different from the Tongan and Samoan systems.[52] Loeb postulates that the idea might be an import from Tonga.[53] The observation by Smith is plausible.

Up until European contact, Niue remained under its own rule. As earlier stated, its government consisted of the king and a council of chiefs. It existed for when the need arose. After the death of King Togia and the establishment of the British Protectorate, the native government institution underwent change.

There was an incident where Tongan warriors attempted to conquer the island but were defeated. A group of Tongan warriors arrived by way of Fakaleaina in Alofi where they were invited by the Niueans to a feast at Anatoga. Unbeknown to the visitors, a large table of food laid before them was set on top of a deep chasm. The visitors who were famished from their long journey hurried to the food but fell into the chasm and perished.[54] The people of Niue have always lived free and independent. In custom, there are no divisions or classifications of people. No one was

49 *supra* note 40, p. 16.

50 *supra* note 8, p. 39. After King Punimata passed, there was an interregnum for a long time; it is not known how many generations lapsed before another was set up.

51 *supra* note 35, art. 54 and art. 55.

52 *supra* note 8, p. 39. Institute of Pacific Studies of the University of the South Pacific and Government of Niue.

53 *supra* note 38. p. 55.

54 Tahafa P. Talagi "Tau Tala Tu Fakaholo A Niue To Hoko Mai e Tau Papalagi" in Terry Chapman et al., *Niue: A History of the Island* (Suva: University of the South Pacific and the Government of Niue,1982), p. 27.

born a slave or king. A person's place in society was dependent on their effort.

The people are of a Polynesian race and speak their own language (Vagahau Niue). There are small variations in the use of words and accent between the villages. The variations have reduced over the years with increased interaction.

The most notable customary traditions and practices are either to do with limiting or allowing access to areas of land and sea for food. A family or village could impose a *fono*[55] or *fakatapu*[56] over land or sea for the purpose of excluding all others or for the purposes of conservation. Sanctuaries for coconut crabs, pigeons, and bats would be *fakatapu* to prevent their depletion. A *fono* could be imposed against persons outside the family or group from accessing resources in their particular area. Depending on the landowners, a *fono* or *fakatapu* imposed could be temporary or permanent.

Certain plants are known to be used during times of drought. To prevent famine, a group would dig *ti* roots scientifically known as the *Cordyline fruticosa*[57] and bake them in an *umu*[58] for three days. The *umu* is large and the *ti* roots would be packaged in large woven coconut baskets. Due to the scale of the work, a *umu ti* is only undertaken as a community effort. The cooked *ti* roots store well and are long lasting. The other crop that is harvested and processed to assist in drought periods is the *pia*[59] scientifically known as *Tacca leontopetaloides*[60] or known as the Polynesian arrowroot. It is known throughout Polynesia as famine food.

There is no surface water on the island. Rainwater was collected using hollowed and cleaned-out whole coconut shells for water catchment. The soil is limestone and in certain areas is red soil. It is porous, causing any rainwater to quickly seep beneath the ground. Because water was scarce, the islanders believed that their king or gods were responsible for rain. These beliefs held true at least until the introduction of Christianity.

The first European contact was by Captain James Cook in June 1774. Cook was on a journey of discovery in the south seas. After several attempts to find a good landing and an entry point to the island, the place was found at Opaahi, Alofi South. However, not long after their arrival at Opaahi, they were met with men holding spears, clubs, and challenging them through war chant. They were met with resistance.[61]

55 Meaning "Prohibition."

56 Meaning "To declare an area sacred ground and closed to others."

57 Temorareo.org, "PPN-Tii."

58 Meaning "Earth oven."

59 Commonly known as the Polynesian arrowroot.

60 Tetiaroa Society, "Polynesian Arrowroot."

61 *supra* note 40, pp. 28–29.

Frustrated with the hostile encounter with the islanders, Cook named Niue "Savage Island." He did not stay long and never returned. He used his extensive knowledge of the Pacific, and although his encounter with the locals was brief and unwelcoming, he compared the Savage Islanders to the Friendly Islanders because of the similarities seen in their canoes and concluded that they were complete and resourceful.[62] Cook achieved his most basic goal of discovering the south sea lands, as well as leaving the enduring impact of recording Niue's exact location on the world map and a description of its formation and typography.[63] These were useful for subsequent seafarers.

Around 1830, the missionary John Williams attempted to make landfall on Niue. He described several instances where his party was met by natives thoroughly equipped for war. Despite this, they did manage to take away two youths, Tupuamana and Uea[64] for the purposes of teaching them religion. He left a negative record of his experience.[65] The youths were taken to Samoa and Raiatea. They were later returned. Uea brought with him "the papaya, the gospel and a disease resembling syphilis."[66] This caused the island to rebel against Uea and his family.

The accounts of why the people of Niue were guarded against contact with visitors have merits. They have a strong aversion to the introduction of infectious disease. Etuata and Tanaki state that

> because of Niue's isolated location and elevated island, this had naturally preserved the health of the people. There were no historical accounts of the devastating impact of disease on the island and the Niueans interacted freely because they were of good health. Therefore, they were very hostile against foreign visitors.[67]

This statement suggests the opposite; it is perhaps a devastating experience with disease that caused the locals to adopt quarantine restrictions to repel visitors.[68]

62 *supra* note 38, p. 34.

63 *supra* note 38, p. 34.

64 *supra* note 35, art. 32 and art.33.

65 John Williams, "Chapter XVII, Leave Aitutaki – Savage Island. In a Narrative of Missionary Enterprises in the South Sea Islands" (Cook Islands Library and Museum Society, 1998), p.78.

66 *supra* note 35.

67 *supra* note 40, p. 22.

68 *supra* note 34, art. 74. "Clearly the people must have at some period of their history have been afflicted with some terrible scourge after the visit of strangers, and this has engendered a fear of all intercourse with outsiders ever since."

Christianity was subsequently introduced to the island in 1846 by the London Missionary Society. The purpose of missions was to introduce the islanders to a better life and replace their "cruel superstitions with law, order, the usages of life and the comforts of civilised life."[69] There is a vast difference between the view of the foreign missionary and the view of the locals about superstitions. Generally, the locals worshipped their own gods as a customary practice to ward off evil and to call upon blessings.[70] There was nothing cruel about it. If anything, the locals' belief in the spiritual realm was helpful for the missionaries. They were a believing people.

After Christianity, settlements gradually dispersed and many were relocated to the coastline and formed villages. It was through Christianity that locals started to learn how to read and write. The teachings of Christianity on sharing and gathering together were easy to adapt to because of the nature of the people. The people were willing and quick to adapt. However, there were still some areas that needed change. The first English missionary to live among the people in 1861 was Rev. George Lawes.[71] By the time of his arrival, many of the villages had their own pastor. Reorganizing and establishing villages and village life were led by the missionaries and this reduced the influence and authority of the king.

Lawes observed that the people struggled to reconcile their customary laws with the rules of Christianity. While many had adopted Christian beliefs, there were still some *Leveki Magafaoa*[72] who were untrustworthy. Recognizing that there needed to be a place to centralize control, a *fono* (council) was formed to discuss and establish law and order. The council consisted of six representatives for each village. Police officers and judges were also appointed to police and enforce the laws.[73] For a time, the locals were law-abiding. There was concern about the increasingly large numbers of young men sailing abroad for work. Due to the increasingly frequent number of ships passing through, it was becoming normal for young men to travel abroad for work. However, they would return with habits that they had picked up from Samoa, Tahiti, Hawaii, Fiji, and Australia.[74] The church regarded them as a bad influence.

69 *supra* note 57, p. 3.

70 *supra* note 38, p. 47. A small part may have been for evil intentions.

71 Fifita Talagi, "Tamaiaga he tau mahani Fakamotu Kehe" in Terry Chapman et al., *Niue: A History of the Island* (Suva: University of the South Pacific and the Government of Niue,1982).

72 Leader appointed by the family. This institution was later recognized in Niuean law.

73 *supra* note 38, p. 40.

74 Ofa Tafatu and I. Tukuitoga, "Tau Faifeau Fakamui mo e Pule Faka Niu Silani" in Terry Chapman et al., *Niue: A History of the Island* (Suva: University of the South Pacific and the Government of Niue,1982), p. 121.

The laws and fines imposed by the *fono*, with the influence of the church, were criticized as prejudiced. They were not crimes recognized by any Christian or civilized community but found in only Polynesia. The young men might have gone away to escape "semi-religious persecution" for offending the moral code of the London Missionary Society. This resulted in driving away many of the best men to Rarotonga and elsewhere.[75]

In late 1862 and early 1863, tragedy struck the island when three Peruvian ships arrived on three different occasions and kidnapped a total of 109 men. They were to be sold as slaves in Peru. Accustomed to ships arriving on the island, the young men would readily load their canoes with supplies and paddle out to trade. The ships did not have to recruit on shore; they simply waited for the islanders who went out to meet them. The islanders were lured on board, held captive, and kidnapped.[76]

Around 1868, a pastor's school was established and the translation of the Bible followed. The translation of the Bible to Niuean was completed by 1900.[77] However, the laws of the council and government system supported by the mission were no longer sufficient to manage the increasingly diverse activities on the island.[78]

For several years and at different times, King Fataiki and King Togia petitioned Queen Victoria for British protection. There was a strong desire for a centralized system of government to deal with domestic and international affairs such as the constant migration of young people offshore, and the increasing number of traders setting up business.[79] Young Niuean men working abroad also needed British protection. Needless to say, the Peruvian slave traffickers who had stolen Niuean men were another bitter experience that urged the various kings' petitions seeking protection for the island itself.

It was not until November 1899 as a consequence of the Samoa Convention[80] that Britain responded favourably to Niue's request. On April 21, 1900, Sir Basil Thompson formally signed the treaty between Britain and Niue followed by the raising of the British flag on Niuean soil for the first time.[81] While Thompson was on the island, he enacted two laws: first, imposing a prohibition on the sale of Niuean land, and

75 W.E. Gudgeon, British Resident, Cook Islands. Despatches from the Governor of New Zealand to the Secretary of State for the Colonies, (Wellington, 1901).

76 H.E. Maude, *Slavers in Paradise, The Peruvian Labour Trade in Polynesia, 1862–1864*, (Canberra: Australian National University Press, 1981).

77 *supra* note 38, p. 42.

78 *supra* note 71, pp. 45–47.

79 *supra* note 8, pp. 140–141.

80 *supra* note 8, p. 142.

81 *supra* note 71, p. 49.

second, the prohibition on the sale of alcohol. Quarantine officers were also appointed to assist with quarantine inspections of visiting vessels.[82]

Unknown to Niue, the British were to hand over Niue and the Cook Islands to New Zealand. Within the same year, on October 19, 1900, Lord Ranfurly visited and signed the treaty for the annexation of Niue to Great Britain.[83] King Togia and 11 chiefs signed, "We, the King and the chiefs of the Island of Niue, do hereby consent to Her Majesty Queen Victoria taking possession of this island and in proof hereof have hereunto subscribed our names this 19th day of October, 1900."[84] By June 11, 1901, a proclamation was issued stating that the Cook Islands and Niue would be administered for Great Britain by New Zealand. Furthermore, it would be administered as a group with the Cook Islands.[85] The locals were taken aback by the sudden change of arrangements.

Subsequently, S. Percy Smith from New Zealand arrived on Niue to commence the establishment of a formal government under the new annexation.[86] After the passing of King Togia and the presence of a Resident Commissioner as the agent for the New Zealand administration, the customary government system was gradually modified and, in some areas, completely replaced. The office of a king was discontinued and a new form of government established. The office of the king had "existed for a 41-year period from 1876 until 1917."[87]

2.3 Culture and Customs of Niue

There are many valuable aspects of Niuean custom and culture responsible for regularizing the functions of Niuean society. However, only matters in relation to the family and Niuean land are dealt with here.

Family is the most basic unit of Niuean society.[88] During the era of missions and the introduction of Christian beliefs, the *patu* were the heads of the *Magafaoa* (family) who would meet with the *iki* (chiefs) to discuss and manage the affairs of the family. A council of chiefs was called to assist the king and to make rules and to take care of the concerns affecting the community. During the discussion of annexation to the British Empire, King Togia and Lord Ranfurly had a meeting for a number of hours. After which the king "insisted the decision be made not by him

82 *supra* note 8, p. 146.
83 *supra* note 8, p. 153.
84 W.E. Gudgeon, British Resident, Cook Islands. Despatches from the Governor of New Zealand to the Secretary of State for the Colonies. 1901.
85 *supra* note 8, pp. 157–158.
86 *supra* note 8, p. 158.
87 *supra* note 8, p. 134.
88 *supra* note 44, p. 11.

alone but in consultation with the *iki* from all the villages."[89] This custom of consulting with each other on significant matters continues today.

In modern society, the family consults and appoints a *Leveki Magafaoa* who is responsible for leading the affairs of the family. The most significant role is in relation to the control of the occupation and use of Niuean land under custom. Ownership of Niuean land is determined by appointing a common ancestor who the family agrees was the original owner of the land and the person from whom their rights derive. In other words, "The Court shall determine the ownership of any land by ascertaining and declaring the *Magafaoa* of that land by reference to the common ancestor of it or by any other means which clearly identifies the *Magafaoa*."[90]

This is followed by the appointment of a *Leveki Magafaoa*. The *Leveki Magafaoa* must consent to the appointment and be agreed to by in writing by a majority of members of the *Magafaoa*. The *Leveki Magafaoa* has a duty to consult with members of the *Magafaoa* in relation to the sale and lease of land or the giving of security charges over land.[91] A *Leveki Magafaoa* has to be a domiciliary[92] of Niue. Members of the *Magafaoa* include members whether resident in Niue or elsewhere.[93]

The constitution defines Niuean land as "land in Niue vested in the Crown but held by Niueans according to the customs and usages of Niue."[94] This is reinforced by legislation where "every title to and estate or interest in Niuean land shall be determined under Niuean custom."[95] Niuean custom regulates the rights and interests of the family in relation to Niuean land.

Custom in relation to Niuean land is rooted in family relationships. Those family relationships are held by knowledge of the genealogy, keeping family traditions, working the land by farming, hunting, and maintaining family presence. Subsistence farming is a key aspect of Niuean custom. Aside from family consumption, taro plantations are used for hosting ceremonies and functions. Hair cutting and ear-piercing ceremonies are major undertakings for families. Although these activities have evolved and have become a form of cultural commerce, it is an expression of Niuean culture that reinforces the nature and identity of Niueans based on the use of Niuean land.

The Land Act 1969 and the Niue Amendment Act (No. 2) 1968 provide the rule in a two-pronged process for the investigation of

89 *supra* note 8, p. 155.
90 Land Act (1969), s. 12.
91 *Ibid.*, s. 15.
92 *Ibid.*, s. 14(5).
93 *Ibid.*, s. 14(2).
94 Constitution of Niue (2019), art. 33 (5).
95 Niue Amendment Act (No 2) (1968), s. 23.

title to Niuean land. These include the determination of title to Niuean land[96] followed by the appointment of a *Leveki Magafaoa*.[97]

In the determination of title to Niuean land, the Land Court has exclusive jurisdiction to investigate the title to Niuean land and to determine the relative interests of owners and occupiers of such land.[98]

The Court refers to the customs and usages of the people as far as it can be ascertained.[99] To assist the Court in investigating the claims, the evidence it requires is a provisional plan or survey of the land,[100] boundaries,[101] grounds of the claim,[102] genealogical tables showing descent from the ancestor or ancestors through whom title is claimed, and all persons admitted by the claimant as entitled with him under the claim;[103] names and approximate location of cultivations, villages, burial places, with the names of relatives of the claimant persons included in the claim who are buried there, and other places or marks of historical interest;[104] and proof or signs of occupation of or connection with the land.[105] Upon the satisfactory provision of evidence, the Court determines the ownership of that land by declaring the *Magafaoa* by naming the common ancestor with whom the *Magafaoa* identifies.

The rules confirm the significance of family as the key unit for preserving custom and culture in the collective ownership and for controlling the occupation and use of land. With collective ownership, parcels of land that are owned by a family could spread over different areas and different villages. For instance, a single person could have interests in parcels of Niuean land on the mother's side and the father's side. On the mother's side, the mother has rights and interests to her mother's and the father's side. On the father's side, the father has rights and interests on his mother's and father's side. As a starting point, therefore, a person has rights in at least four different genealogical lines. A person's rights and interests to Niuean land could be established or removed depending on whom the Court determines as the *Magafaoa* or common ancestor of the land. For this reason, the identification of the common ancestor is often disputed.

In the case of a dispute as to who should be declared *Magafaoa*, Judge Carter in 2009 clarified: "while individual occupation and exercise of

96 *supra* note 90, s. 10.
97 *supra* note 90, s. 14.
98 *supra* note 95, s. 22.
99 *supra* note 90, s. 10(1).
100 *supra* note 90, s. 10(2).
101 *supra* note 90, s. 11(a).
102 *supra* note 90, s. 11(b).
103 *supra* note 90, s. 11(c).
104 *supra* note 90, s. 11(d).
105 *supra* note 90, s. 11(e).

other customary rights may influence the Court in its determination of the *magafaoa*, the focus is on the family or group and not on the determination of individual rights."[106] Another common land dispute is when both applicants have genealogical links but one family competes for full ownership to the exclusion of the other. When the Court has considered all the evidence based on genealogy, occupation and use, it will seek to reach a decision that is fair to both parties. In the case of *Tutavaha v. Manukuo (2008)* Justice Isaac stated

> After considering all the evidence, I find both parties have genealogical ties to this land. I also find that this land by family arrangement has been occupied by both families in past years. The Tutavaha Jackson family have had land titled in Block A of approximately 2,645 square metres by consent of the parties. It seems only fair and reasonable that the other side of the family who have also occupied this land for generations should also receive a portion of it.[107]

Decisions made unilaterally and without consultation with and the consent of the *Magafaoa* are another common point of dispute in Niuean land. Internal disputes among families have often led to applications made to the Court. However, the Court has made it clear that consultation should take place. A *Leveki Magafaoa* has a duty to consult the *Magafaoa* on matters pertaining to the land. For instance, there is a case where the *Leveki Magafaoa* issued a trespass notice on another member of the *Magafaoa* via the police. The Court rejected the trespass notice and ordered the police to withdraw the note. The Court stated that

> It must be remembered that in Niue, no individual owns land. Land is vested in a common ancestor for the benefit of the ancestor's descendants. In this situation and given the Niuean land tenure system and the wider consideration of the Court is required to examine, including the requirement for the *Leveki Magafaoa* to consult the *Magafaoa*. The *magafaoa* should look to resolve the issues rather than have the Court resolve it for them.[108]

One question that often arises concerning the duty of the *Leveki Magafaoa* to consult the *Magafaoa* is who should be consulted and who should not. The law provides that the *Leveki Magafaoa* "shall under custom consult

106 *Hekau v. Tongahai* Niue Legislation Supplement 2008/2009 (Government of Niue 2008/2009), p. 119.
107 *Tutavaha v. Manukuo* (2008) Niue LR, p. 187.
108 *Fetaui v. Police* (2020) Niue LR, p. 1489.

with members of the *Magafaoa* whether resident in Niue or elsewhere."[109] In *Koligi v. Iakopo*, in respect of the consultation rule per Section 15 of the Land Act 1969, the Court highlighted that

> the *Leveki Magafaoa* has an obligation to consult with members of the *Magafaoa* in exercising their powers regarding the occupation and use of the land. That section also provides that the *leveki magafaoa* must consult with members whether they are resident in Niue or elsewhere. Any suggestion that Ms Iakopo has a greater entitlement over other members of the *Magafaoa* by virtue of being resident on the land in Niue, or a lesser obligation to consult with the *Magafaoa* not resident in Niue, does not hold weight.[110]

At the very least, if the *Leveki Magafaoa* can show that he has undertaken consultation with a majority of the members of the *Magafaoa*, the fact that he failed to consult one specific member is "not sufficiently serious to warrant a removal of the Leveki."[111] The Court also emphasized that "Niuean custom is inclusive, not exclusive."[112]

The role of the *Leveki Magafaoa* is as the legal administrator of the land.[113] There is a common misconception that *Leveki* can be easily challenged, removed, or replaced whenever a member of the *Magafaoa* disagrees with a decision. For instance, the number of applications to the Land Court to grant an injunction against actions of a *Leveki Magafaoa* is high. The applications range from any number of things; for example: an injunction to prevent the building of a house, demolishing a house, burying a deceased relative, clearing and planting on land, halting all church activities on land, preventing development on land.

Without professional legal assistance, applicants waste time and resources on making complaints to the Court rather than first seeking legal assistance before doing so or, at the very least, resorting to the customary rule of consulting each other. Referring to the Court should be sought as a last resort.

109 *supra* note 90, s. 15.
110 *Koligi v. Iakopo* (2017) Niue LR, p. 1003.
111 *Laifone v. Tauekipaoa* (2019) Niue LR, p. 1411.
112 *supra* note 107.
113 *Talafasi and Others v. Hipa and Togiakona* (2023) Niue LR, p. 13.

2.4 Niue in Global Society and the Relationship with New Zealand

On June 11, 1901, New Zealand passed the *Cook, etc. Islands Boundaries and Inclusion in New Zealand Proclamation 1901.*[114] Thus began New Zealand's presence in Niue through its agent, the Resident Commissioner. The first Resident Commissioner organized the election of the first Island Council consisting of representatives for each village.[115] The transition into a new government order was established under the Cook and Other Islands Government Act 1901.[116] Niue was a territory of New Zealand included with the Cook Islands.

The Cook Islands Act 1901 was repealed and replaced by the Cook Islands Act 1915. The later Act established the executive government, the Island Council, the High Court, and the Land Court. It was not until after the Cook Islands voted for its self-government in 1965 that the New Zealand Parliament enacted laws specific to Niue.

Political change started in the 1960s when the United Nations recognized that the people of colonial territories had a right to complete freedom, sovereignty, and the integrity of their national territory. A declaration was made urging the end of colonialism and encouraging non-self-governing territories and territories to exercise their own powers to self-govern.[117]

In 1962, New Zealand conformed with the resolution and consulted with the Cook Islands and Niue to decide their future. There were three propositions set forth for Niue to consider, namely: independence, some form of self-government, or full integration with New Zealand.[118]

The Cook Islands achieved self-government in free association with New Zealand on August 4, 1965. Niue, being anxious about her future, agreed to consider her options but wanted to decide in her own time. "There was a strongly negative reaction to the suggestion that Niue's progress to self-government should be rapid or should follow a prearranged timetable."[119]

114 By Order in Council dated May 13, 1901 under the Colonial Boundaries Act 1895 (Imp) *1 New Zealand Gazette 1307.*

115 *supra* note 8, p. 163.

116 Cook and Other Islands Government, "An Act to Provide Temporary for the Government of the Cook and Other Islands in the Pacific within the Boundaries of the Colony of New Zealand" (1904), No. 44.

117 United Nations General Assembly, *Resolution 1514 (XV) Office of the High Commissioner Declaration on the Granting of Independence to Colonial Countries and Peoples* (December 14, 1960).

118 Prof. R.Q. Quentin-Baxter "Report on the Constitution Development of Niue" (Government of Niue, 1971), p. 3.

119 *Ibid.*

Consequently, the New Zealand government gave assurances that the "Government and people of Niue retain the right to determine the pace of their constitutional development."[120]

After several rounds of consultations and persuasion, it took a lot to prepare the people to determine their own future.[121] It seems that the events in 1900 and 1901 might have made the people extra cautious. This time, Niue wanted the change to be on their own terms.[122] On October 19, 1974, Niue became a self-governing state in free association with New Zealand.

It took another 33 years before Niue could step outside of her comfort zone and assert self-government through building her international legal personality. In December 2007, Niue signed diplomatic relations on her own behalf with a state that was not New Zealand or the UK. Niue commenced diplomatic ties with China. The two governments aspired to protect, retain, and develop the culture of Niue and to engage to the greatest possible extent in international and regional events. As of August 2024, Niue has entered into 26 diplomatic relations with other states, not counting the treaty with Britain in 1900 and the New Zealand Proclamation in 1901.

2.5 Current Challenges Faced by Niue

Among all the challenges Niue experienced over time, it appears that the constant challenge from as far back as the late 1840s with young Niuean men was regular travel abroad for work. The people adapted very quickly. They sought economic advancement by emigration to New Zealand during annexation, and that continued after the constitutional achievements of October 19, 1974. In fact, it was one of the requirements before the referendum in 1974 that New Zealand citizenship was retained. Quentin-Baxter emphasized that

> If the small community of Niue is to have a life of its own, and to resist the drift of population, it must build up its own institutions of government. These in turn can give the people of Niue the will to make progress, with New Zealand assistance in the economic, social and educational fields.[123]

120 *Ibid.*
121 *Ibid.*, pp. 5–6.
122 *Ibid.*, p. 2.
123 *supra* note 118, para 60.

Niue offers the advantages of having open spaces, a clean environment and a peaceful lifestyle. However, it lacks the population necessary to maintain and offer quality essential services. While the services offered by the system may not be overburdened, the workers themselves, who have had to take on many responsibilities and work in small teams or in isolation, are overburdened.

In an increasingly interconnected world, Niue's social, political, and legal responsibilities are no longer confined to domestic issues. It is now a small island developing state in a fast-changing world.

References

Literature

Chapman, Terry et al., *Niue: A History of the Island* (Suva: University of the South Pacific and the Government of Niue, 1982).

Cook and other Islands Government, "An Act to Provide Temporary for the Government of the Cook and Other Islands in the Pacific within the Boundaries of the Colony of New Zealand" (1904), No. 44. available at: <https://www7.austlii.edu.au/nz/legis/hist_act/caoiga19011ev1901n44425.pdf>.

Etuata, I. and P. Tanaki, "Tau Atua Tuai he Motu ko Niue he Vaha Pouli," in Terry Chapman et al., *Niue: A History of the Island* (Suva: University of the South Pacific and the Government of Niue, 1982).

Gardner, R.O., *Trees and Shrubs of Niue* (Auckland: Katsura, 2011).

Geodatos.net, "Distance from Cook Islands to Niue." available at: <https://www.geodatos.net/en/distances/countries/from-niue-to-cook-islands>, accessed July 29, 2025.

Geodatos.net, "Distance from Tonga to Niue." available at: <https://www.geodatos.net/en/distances/countries/from-tonga-to-niue>, accessed July 29, 2025.

Geodatos.net, "Distance from Niue to Samoa." available at: <https://www.geodatos.net/en/distances/countries/from-niue-to-samoa>, accessed July 29, 2025.

Government of Niue, "National Biodiversity Strategy and Action Plan 2015" (2015), available at: <https://www.cbd.int/doc/world/nu/nu-nbsap-v2-en.pdf>.

Government of Niue, Statistics and Immigration Office, Ministry of Finance and Planning "Statistical Release: Niue Census of Population and Housing, Preliminary Report" (2022), available at: <https://niuestatistics.nu/population/niue-census-of-population-and-housing-2022/>, accessed July 29, 2025.

Government of Niue, Ministry of Finance and Planning, "Health Indicators 1987–1991." available at: <https://niuestatistics.nu/category/social/health/>, accessed July 29, 2025.

Government of Niue, Ministry of Finance and Planning, "Health Indicators 2012–2016." available at: <https://niuestatistics.nu/category/social/health/>, accessed July 29, 2025.

Gudgeon, W.E., "British Resident, Cook Islands. Despatches from the Governor of New Zealand to the Secretary of State for the Colonies." (Wellington, 1901), available at: <https://paperspast.natlib.govt.nz/parliamentary/AJHR1901-I.2.1.2.1>, accessed July 29, 2025.

Hekau, Maihetoe and Vilisoni Kumitau, "'o e Tupuaga he tau Tagata Niue," in Terry Chapman et al., *Niue: A History of the Island* (Suva: University of the South Pacific and the Government of Niue, 1982).

Latitude.to, "Satellite Map of Niue." available at: <https://latitude.to/satellite-map/nu/niue/762/niue>, accessed July 29, 2025.

Loeb, Edwin M., *History and Traditions of Niue*. Bernice P. Bishop Museum, Bulletin 32 (Honolulu, 1926).

Maude, H.E., *Slavers in Paradise, The Peruvian Labour Trade in Polynesia, 1862–1864* (Australian National University Press, 1981).

New Zealand Gazette, "New Zealand Gazette 1307." (June 13, 1901), available at: < https://library.victoria.ac.nz/databases/nzgazettearchive/pubs/gazettes/1901/1901%20ISSUE%20059.pdf>.

Niue Climate Change Project, "Niue Island Initial National Communication, United Nations Framework Convention on Climate Change" (2000), available at: <https://unfccc.int/sites/default/files/resource/Niue%20INC.pdf>.

Niue Health Department and World Health Organisation, *NCD Risk Factors Steps Report* (2013).

Niue Statistics, "Niue Census of Population and Housing, 2022." available at: <https://niuestatistics.nu/population/niue-census-of-population-and-housing-2022/>, accessed July 29, 2025.

Pacific-Australia Climate Change Science and Adaptation Planning Program, "Current and Future Climate of Niue." available at: <https://www.pacificclimatechangescience.org/wp-content/uploads/2013/06/12_PACCSAP-Niue-11pp_WEB.pdf>.

Pointer, Margaret, *Niue 1774–1974, 200 Years of Contact and Change* (Otago: Otago University Press, 2015).

Quentin-Baxter, R.Q., "Report on the Constitution Development of Niue" (1971), Government of Niue.

Smith, S. Percy, *Niue the Island and Its People* (Suva: University of the South Pacific, 1983 [Originally published 1902]).

South Pacific Community, "Niue." available at: <https://www.spc.int/our-members/niue/details>, accessed July 29, 2025.

Sykes, W.R., *Contributions to the Flora of Niue* (N.Z. Department of Science & Industrial Research Bull, 1970).

Tafatu, Ofa and I. Tukuitoga, "Tau Faifeau Fakamui mo e Pule Faka Niu Silani," in Terry Chapman et al., *Niue: A History of the Island* (Suva: University of the South Pacific and the Government of Niue, 1982).

Talagi, Fifita, "Tamaiaga he tau mahani Fakamotu Kehe," in Terry Chapman et al., *Niue: A History of the Island* (Suva: University of the South Pacific and the Government of Niue, 1982).

Talagi, Tahafa P., "Tau Tala Tu Fakaholo A Niue To Hoko Mai e Tau Papalagi," in Terry Chapman et al., *Niue: A History of the Island* (Suva: University of the South Pacific and the Government of Niue, 1982).

Temarareo.org, "PPN-Tii." available at: <https://www.temarareo.org/PPN-Tii.html>, accessed July 29, 2025.

Tetiaroa Society, "Polynesian Arrowroot." available at: <https://www.tetiaroasociety.org/island/plants/polynesian-arrowroot>, accessed July 29, 2025.

United Nations General Assembly, *Resolution 1514 (XV) Office of the High Commissioner Declaration on the Granting of Independence to Colonial Countries and Peoples* (December 14, 1960).

Vilitama, Hafè, "Ko e Fakatufono Motu he Vaha i Tuai i Niue," in Terry Chapman et al., *Niue: A History of the Island* (Suva: University of the South Pacific and the Government of Niue, 1982).

Whistler, W.A., *Notes on the Flora of Niue* (N.Z Journal of Botany, 1984).

Whistler, W.A., *The Rare Plants of Niue* (Honolulu, Hawaii: Isle Botanica, 2013).

Williams, John, "Chapter XVII, Leave Aitutaki – Savage Island. In *a Narrative of Missionary Enterprises in the South Sea Islands*" (1998), Cook Islands Library and Museum Society.

Yuncker, G.G., *The Flora of Niue Island* (B.P. Bishop Museum Bull, 1943).

Interviews

CEO of Telecom Niue Limited, June 2025.

Cases

Fetaui v. Police (2020) Niue LR 1489.

Hekau v. Tongahai Niue Legislation Supplement 2008/2009 (Government of Niue 2008/2009) 119.

Koligi v. Iakopo (2017) Niue LR 1003.

Laifone v. Tauekipaoa (2019) Niue LR 1411.

Talafasi and Others v. Hipa and Togiakona (2023) Niue LR 13.

Tutavaha v. Manukuo (2008) Niue LR 187.

Legislation

Constitution of Niue .

Cook and Other Islands Government Act 1901 (1901).

Cook Islands Act 1915 (1915).

Interpretation Act (2004).

Land Act (1969).

Letters Patent Constituting the Office of the Governor General of New Zealand 1983/225.

Maritime Zones Act (2013).

Niue Amendment Act (No. 2) (1968).

Niue Assembly Act (1966).

Niue Constitution Act (1974).
Niue Moana Mahu Marine Protected Area Regulations (2020).
Taoga Niue Act (2012).
Village Councils Act (2016).
Warrant Declaring Land to Be Roads (1971).

3 Law and Justice in Niue

Kahealani Sinahemana Hekau

3.1 History of Legal Developments on Niue

The ancient society of Niue was controlled by beliefs in the supernatural or spirits and gods thought to control the environment and the weather. The people worshipped gods who were once men, the sky, the wind, sun, moon, rainbow, and other living sacred land or sea creatures. Customs and practices around these beliefs eventually formed the rules for where or when to go hunting, fishing, gathering, planting, harvesting, or how to protect against fatal enemies. The close connection with nature meant that the rules sought a balance between use and conservation. Customary rules and usages inherently promote the sustainable use of resources. For example, a *tapu* or a prohibition could be placed over a particular area to prevent harvesting, taking, or hunting. A *fono* is a prohibition against trespass over land that is left fallow to naturally regenerate, or a *fono* may simply be a customary practice notifying a prohibition against trespassing on the land. These measures prevent overuse and overharvesting to allow nature to replenish for the use of future generations.

Due to the oral nature of Niuean custom, the rules were unwritten. Hence, an oral legal system prevailed. Some records of the rules can be found in chants and songs. Chants were often prayers for blessings and forms of worship. Songs were means of praise and celebrations. Chants, songs and dances were mediums that document and preserve the knowledge of names of gods, places, practices or the enforcement of rules.

From the late 1800s up until British protection in 1900, rules were determined by the elders or heads of each family. The elders in a group formed the local council for each village, which would assist the king. The purpose of the rules focused on the protection of the family unit and ensuring its survival by controlling access to food resources on land and the sea. Ownership of land was determined and controlled by the family as a collective.

Family groups were scattered in settlements and forts that were located inland. Despite the difficult terrain, the inland settlements were sheltered until at least 1870 when most of the settlements relocated to the coastline

DOI: 10.4324/9781003585688-3

and formed villages.[1] The relocation of settlements as influenced by the church was for the purposes of church gatherings, planning, and social order. Local laws promulgated by the chiefs and rulers of the island were in force for years but were unwritten until, with the assistance of the English missionary Rev F.E. Lawes in 1875,[2] the first laws were drafted and written down.

On April 21, 1900, a treaty for British protection was signed on Niue between King Togia and the British envoy Basil Thompson.[3] Before departure, Basil Thompson endorsed two laws against the sale of land and the sale of liquor.[4]

At the assembly of the king, chiefs, and rulers of Niue, a revised law was passed on June 5, 1900.[5] The law dealt with stealing, cheating, lost property, destruction of property, arson, assault, quarrelling, minor offences, drunkenness, fornication, adultery, eloping with another man's wife, visiting ships for immoral purposes, abducting women to ships, procuring abortion, and Niuean land.

Several months later on October 19, 1900, a Treaty of Annexation was signed between King Togia and eleven council members with the visiting Lord Ranfurly.[6] Niue became formally part of the British Empire. Unknown to Niue, Britain had other obligations to attend to with New Zealand. New Zealand was eager to gain greater influence in the Pacific. To satisfy New Zealand's desire for greater influence, a Proclamation by an Order in Council declared the Cook group and "other" islands and territories part of the New Zealand Colony. The New Zealand Parliament was granted "temporary provision for the administration of the Government in the said islands."[7]

All of this happened independent of Niue's knowledge, request, or consent. New Zealand now gained administrative powers over it. Compounding the problem, Niue was administered as part of the Cook Islands under the Cook and Other Islands Government Act 1901.[8] There were vast differences between the two countries; Niue was a standalone

1 Ofa Tafatu and Ianeta Joylynn Tukuitonga, "Developments to Annexation" in Terry Chapman et al., *Niue: A History of the Island*, Government of Niue and (Suva: University of the South Pacific and Government of Niue, 1982), p. 122.

2 Edwin M. Loeb, *History and Traditions of Niue* (Bernice P. Bishop Museum, Bulletin 32, Honolulu, Hawaii, 1926), p. 39.

3 Margaret Pointer, Niue *1774–1974 200 Years of Contact and Change* (Otago: Otago University Press, 2015), p. 143.

4 *supra* note 3, p. 146.

5 Laws of Niue 1901, *Appendix to the Journals of the House of Representatives* 1902, Session 1, A-03.

6 *supra* note 3, pp. 155–156.

7 Cook and Other Islands Government Act 1901, No. 44.

8 *supra* note 7.

island while the Cook Islands were a group of islands spread over a great maritime area requiring inter-island interaction. There was little travel and communication between Niue and the Cook Islands. They had been annexed by Britain earlier, which gave them some experience of being a British protectorate. Meanwhile, Niue was declared a British protectorate and annexed within a short span of less than a year.

The law of the new administration recognized the existence of local laws, customs, and usages and provided for their continuation so long as they aligned with the general principles of humanity. The new law also provided for:

(i) the operation of New Zealand law so far as expedient for the peace, order, good government, and welfare of residents,[9]
(ii) the provision for the extension to the islands of the jurisdiction of courts of justice,[10]
(iii) the appointment of a Resident Commissioner as the representative of the New Zealand government to administer government on the islands,[11]
(iv) the establishment by the governor of a tribunal for ascertaining and determining title to native land and differentiating titles acquired by native custom and usage from titles otherwise lawfully acquired,[12]
(v) the continuation on Niue of the Island Council to be known as the Niue Island Council,[13]
(vi) grant of enactment making powers to the Island Council to make local ordinances for the government and welfare of the residents[14] with assent of the governor,[15]
(vii) the payment of customs duties on all importation of goods[16] and establishment of public revenues for payment of public expenditures,[17] and
(viii) the grant of powers to the governor to set aside reserves of land for navy and military purposes.[18]

9 *supra* note 7, s. 3.
10 *supra* note 7, s. 4.
11 *supra* note 7, s. 5.
12 *supra* note 7, s. 6.
13 *supra* note 7, s. 7.
14 *supra* note 7, s. 8.
15 *supra* note 7, s. 9.
16 *supra* note 7, s. 10.
17 *supra* note 7, s. 14.
18 *supra* note 7, s. 15

Thus, the new law established a Resident Commissioner over the Cook Islands group with overarching powers. What this meant for Niue was to gradually take away all authority and recognition of the office of a king. All treaties for British protection and the Treaty of Annexation had been previously discussed with and signed by King Togia. Recognition of the local authority in the new law was given to the Island Council and with the role of the king as its president.[19] In September 1901, S. Percy Smith was appointed by New Zealand as the Acting Resident Agent on Niue. His immediate tasks were to establish the government administration and draft local legislation.[20] He first dealt with transitional matters such as the continuation of the King's Council for a year and the recognition of local law. In October 1901, at the meeting of the king and council and with the approval of the Resident Agent, five new laws were passed. They included the:

(i) Niue Council Act 1901.[21] This law provided for the continuation of the first council for one year and thereafter subsequent members would be elected for a term of three years.[22] The king was President of the Council, which would summon and preside over meetings and sign all laws, regulations, and orders of the council.

(ii) Revenue of Niue Act 1901.[23] This law provided for the raising of public revenue from customs duties, fees, fines, and other moneys payable by enactment. An audit of the Revenue of Niue Account would be carried out by an auditor appointed by the Governor of New Zealand.

(iii) Native Magistrates and Police Act 1901[24] established a court to determine complaints of breaches of the law enacted by the Council. The local court had no jurisdiction over breaches by white people.[25]

(iv) Marriage, Divorce, and Registration Act 1901[26] established the legal age for marriage. The legal age for men was 21 years and for women 15 years. Marriages were recognized only if carried out by

19 *supra* note 3, p. 163.

20 *supra* note 3, p. 158.

21 Appendix to the Journals of the House of Representatives, p. 33.

22 *Ibid.*; Niue Council Act 1901, Section 2.

23 *supra* note 21, p. 34.

24 *supra* note 21, p. 35.

25 Section 1. Be it therefore enacted by the Council of Niue that all cases of breaches of the law shall be dealt with under this Act: Provided that in all cases where white people are concerned the native Magistrates hereafter mentioned shall have no jurisdiction (…).

26 *supra* note 21, p. 37.

a licensed minister of religion and by native pastors registered with the Resident Agent.

(v) Emigration Act 1901[27] established the rules for regularizing labour migration. No person under the age of 16 was allowed to enter into a labour agreement with a foreign white person and no persons could be absent for more than a year. Persons emigrating for other reasons were required to show evidence that their dependants left behind would be adequately provided for.

The first Resident Agent spent just over three months on Niue establishing the New Zealand administration government system. Despite being competent in his work, he had great difficulties communicating with the local population. He stated that "it was difficult work explaining laws with an imperfect knowledge of the language."[28] He recommended that any successor who would follow him should learn to speak Niuean.[29]

Under the Cook and Other Islands Government Act Amendment Act 1903, a Resident Commissioner[30] was appointed specifically for Niue, and the New Zealand Supreme Court could hear appeals from a decision of any court held in Niue.[31]

A more elaborate Cook Islands Act 1915 and the Cook Islands Amendment Act 1957 were enacted to provide for an executive government, legislation-making powers, powers of the Resident Commissioner, and laws in relation to different sectors. The usual forms of punishment were hard labour and the construction of public roads.

King Togia died in 1917.[32] There was no formal acknowledgement in law or continuation of the office of the king under the new administration.

The Island Council with the approval of the Resident Commissioner had the overall authority over Niue government affairs. The Resident Agent, and later the Resident Commissioner who succeeded S. Percy Smith, was Christopher Maxwell from 1901 to 1907. He was described as a hands-on man who engaged in infrastructure development, building roads and water reservoirs.[33] The next Resident Commissioner, Henry Cornwall who served from 1907 to 1917, continued with infrastructure development and trade. In 1909, he supported the building of the first

27 *supra* note 21, p. 38.

28 Dick Scott, *Would a Good Man Die? Niue Islands, New Zealand and the Late Mr Larsen* (Auckland: Hodder & Stoughton, 1993), p. 20.

29 *supra* note 28, p. 21.

30 Cook and Other Islands Act Amendment 1903, s. 4.

31 *supra* note 30, s. 5.

32 *supra* note 2, p. 44.

33 *supra* note 3, pp. 178–179.

public school, Tufukia.[34] Land was acquired for the development of the wharf, residences, and a jail. In trade, copra and woven hats were major export commodities. In 1916, the first traffic law was promulgated: the Traffic Regulation Ordinance 1916.[35]

From 1916 to 1959, the Island Council promulgated 60 laws.[36] From 1959 to 1974, the Niue Island Assembly promulgated 93 laws.[37] Key legislation from that era that is still in force in 2025 are the Electric Power Supply Act 1960, Income Tax Act 1961, Public Health Act 1965, and two land statutes.

The rule of law had different impacts on the local population depending on the personality of the Resident Commissioner. Many Resident Commissioners were ex-soldiers[38] and were particularly hard on breakers of morality and liquor consumption laws. In 1950 during the rule of Resident Commissioner Hector Larsen, a total of 1,256 convictions were imposed under the Cook Islands Act on a population of less than 5,000.[39] Prison sentences were excessive and a conviction to manual labour was no longer for the building of public roads only, but for manual labour at the Resident Commissioner's residence, the prison farm, and the golf course.[40]

Larsen's obsession with power caused him to discount the authority and relevance of the Island Council. "He never tired of reminding the Council that it had signed away its powers with the annexation."[41] This was clearly misleading. Could this have been because the laws were not translated into Niuean, not made available to them in written copy, nor were they given any legal assistance? The Island Council made several inquiries as to how much longer Larsen had remaining on the island.[42]

In 1953, Resident Commissioner Larsen was murdered by three Niuean prisoners. His death was described by historian Dick Scott as negligence by New Zealand. "Responsibility sits with the island territories department who left him largely to his own devices and with the public service commission who failed to carry out the staff supervision that it is its duty to perform."[43]

34 *supra* note 3, p. 184.
35 *supra* note 3, p. 188.
36 Chronological table of Statutes, Niue Laws, 2006, Vol. 1, p. xxxi
37 *Ibid.*, p. xxxiv
38 *supra* note 28, p. 25, p. 28, and p. 30. Resident Commissioners Guy N. Morris 1918–1921, 1922–1925, Captain Luckham 1923–1931, and Captain Bell 1931–1941.
39 *supra* note 28, p. 51.
40 *supra* note 28, p. 72.
41 *supra* note 28, p. 64.
42 *supra* note 28, p. 67.
43 *supra* note 28, p. 13.

Larsen's successor was Jock McEwen, whose approach to the role was very different. He served for three years from 1953 to 1956. His heart was in the right place. He took time to learn Niuean, and at his first meeting with the Island Council, he uttered a few sentences in Niuean, to which the result was electric.[44] At the end of McEwen's service, the Island Council regained its confidence, and members were able to express their views freely.[45] After Niue, McEwen became the New Zealand Secretary of Island Territories in 1958. He supported the building of concrete homes following the 1959 and 1960 cyclones,[46] assisted with the consultations on constitutional developments in 1965,[47] and initiated the approval of the airport construction in 1968.[48] Concerned with the growing issues around land tenure, he started drafting the law for tenure in Niuean land in his spare time. He accurately pointed out that Niue's land system was based on social custom, which had evolved over the centuries. In summary, he provided that[49]

> Niue needed a system of registered titles, to provide certainty of ownership and identification of each piece of land. In Niue the unit of land ownership was the *magafaoa*, the line of descent or family, usually consisting of several generations descending from one man and woman. The head of the family, usually the senior male descendant of the original owner, was the pule *magafaoa* or family ruler. This position was not hereditary; the family chose their leader, who could be deposed by them. The pule *magafaoa* had the final say on land matters, but always had to consult with the family, before making a decision. When the family increased, the pule *magafaoa* could divide the land between different branches of the family and create new pule *magafaoa* to manage each part of that land. Under this system, land tenure depended on occupation, and of people moved away, their land fell back into the pool of family land and could be allocated to someone else.

In 1968, the Niue Amendment Act No. 2 was enacted to deal with land tenure, Crown land, Niuean land, land for church purposes, roads, and the Land Court. In 1969, the Land Act was enacted to establish a registration

44 Mary McEwen *To Oka – Pakeha Kaumatua, The Life of Jock McEwen* (Wellington: Riverisco Trust, 2016), p. 92.

45 *supra* note 44, p. 117.

46 *supra* note 44, p. 144.

47 R.Q. Quentin-Baxter, "Report on the Constitutional Development of Niue" (Government of Niue, 1971), p. 3.

48 *supra* note 44, p. 142.

49 *supra* note 44, p. 146.

system. The law deals with registration, investigation of title, appointment of a *Leveki Magafaoa*, the different types of alienation of Niuean land, leases, occupation orders, security charges, partitions, exchanges, sales, reservations, surveys, and others. The procedure for the sale of Niuean land only to the Crown was provided under Section 43. These pieces of legislation have withstood the test of time and remain as the basis for determining ownership of Niuean land and resolving land disputes.

In the short period of time that Niue was annexed by New Zealand, the focus was entirely on the establishment of a New Zealand system, removal of the kingship, and ensuring the power of the Resident Commissioner, with very little attention to the people and their language as the medium of communication and the key to understanding customary law and practice. There was no opportunity for Niue to formally convey its views against the sudden change of circumstances imposed on them by the annexation by New Zealand. Such initial circumstances would have been unacceptable under the modern principle of self-determination.[50] What happened fell short of the standard where a people have the right to determine their political status and to freely pursue their economic, social, and cultural development.

By the late 1960s, Niue seemed to have accepted, in hindsight, the presence of New Zealand.

3.2 The Constitution of Niue

As a result of the United Nations Declaration on the Granting of Independence to Colonial Countries and Peoples, New Zealand, in 1962, consulted the Cook Islands and Niue about their future status. The Cook Islands opted for self-government in free association with New Zealand in 1965. This marked the enactment of the Niue Act 1966, which established key aspects of the Government of Niue. Separate from the Cook Islands, Niue needed time to carefully consider its options. Niue needed reassurance on three key factors, that is:[51]

(i) Niueans would retain New Zealand citizenship;
(ii) Receive assurance that New Zealand would keep its financial administrative aid to enable maintenance of an acceptable standard of living; and
(iii) Have the ability to determine its own terms.

50 United Nations Human Rights "Office of the High Commissioner Declaration on the Granting of Independence to Colonial Countries and Peoples" General Assembly Resolution 1514 (XV) 1960.

51 *supra* note 47, p. 2.

The Niuean people needed a lot of reassurance and took at least twelve years to make a decision. The point was that "there can be no real constitutional progress if the people of Niue are deeply divided about their basic objectives."[52] Worries about economic and social development and of emigration persisted in the minds of the people. It cannot be ignored that perhaps the Niue Assembly was overly cautious towards New Zealand because of the annexation incident in 1901. At village meetings[53]

> many people considered that it was far too soon to take up again the question of constitutional development. There was, they insisted no reason at all why Niue should follow in the footsteps of other Pacific territories, whose situations were quite different from their own. Why should New Zealand, knowing Niue's weakness, wish to enforce such anxious decisions upon the Niuean people: was it because of international pressures?

In 1974, New Zealand enacted the Niue Constitution Act 1974. The Act secured Niue's desire to be self-governing,[54] declaration of the Constitution as the supreme law of Niue,[55] retained British nationality and New Zealand citizenship,[56] New Zealand continued responsibility over external affairs and defence,[57] and New Zealand continued to provide necessary economic and administrative assistance to Niue[58] and the requirement for positive cooperation between the prime minister of New Zealand and the premier of Niue.[59] It also required a New Zealand representative to be stationed on Niue on behalf of the Government of New Zealand.[60]

The Constitution of Niue covers eight parts. Part 1 establishes the executive Government of Niue, which comprises the executive authority vested in Her Majesty the Queen in right of New Zealand and the Governor-General of New Zealand as Her Majesty's representative in relation to Niue. It established a Cabinet of Ministers comprising the prime minister and three members from the Niue Assembly. Cabinet is collectively responsible. Part 2 establishes the legislative Government of Niue, comprising a speaker elected by members of the assembly. The

52 *supra* note 47, p. 9.
53 *supra* note 47, p. 4.
54 Niue Constitution Act 1974, Government of Niue, s. 3.
55 *supra* note 54, s. 4.
56 *supra* note 54, s. 5.
57 *supra* note 54, s. 6.
58 *supra* note 54, s. 7.
59 *supra* note 54, s. 8.
60 *supra* note 54, s. 9.

assembly is comprised of elected representatives for each of the 14 villages and 6 members elected by the combined total constituencies to a common roll seat. Part 3 establishes the judiciary and the appointment of justices of the peace, commissioners, and judges of the High Court, a High Court, a Court of Appeal, and refers to the Privy Council. Part 4 deals with the public revenues of Niue. Part 5 establishes different sectors of health, education, and social services. Part 6 establishes a public service. Part 7 has transitional provisions, and Part 8 is the interpretation of terms.

In respect of Niue culture and custom, Article 23 described Niuean and English as the official languages of the Niue Assembly. In Article 33, any proposed bill that would affect customary title to Niuean land, the alienation of Niuean land, or the purchase or acquisition of Niuean land cannot proceed unless accompanied by a report of a Commission of Inquiry. Special provisions also exist for any bill that would affect the Public Service; the speaker will require such a bill to be accompanied by a report by the Niue Public Service Commission outlining the legal, constitutional, and policy issues of the bill.

The Constitution of Niue is a neat model for small jurisdictions. It is unique in a way that all of its provisions are entrenched. Ten provisions are doubly entrenched. Any changes to the Constitution require the affirmative vote of two thirds of the members of the assembly and thereafter the affirmative vote of a simple majority of the people. A double entrenchment is where an affirmative vote of two thirds majority is required at the assembly and the people in respect of changes to Sections 2–9 of the Niue Constitution Act 1974 and Articles 1 and 69 of the Constitution. The method for amending the Constitution is provided by Article 35 and is as follows:

Power of the Niue Assembly to repeal or amend this Constitution

(1) A Bill repealing or amending or modifying or extending any of the provisions of the Niue Constitution Act 1974 or of this Constitution or making any provision consistent with any of those provisions shall become law if, and only if –

(a) It has been passed by the Niue Assembly in compliance with the following requirements –

(i) On both the final reading, and on the reading, which preceded it, the Bill receives the affirmative votes of not less than two-thirds of the total membership of the Assembly, as provided in Article 16(2)(b) of this Constitution; and

(ii) The vote on the final reading takes place at least 13 weeks after but excluding the day of the vote on the reading which preceded it; and

(b) It has thereafter submitted to a poll, conducted in a manner prescribed by law, of the persons who at the time of that poll were entitled to vote as electors at a general election of members of the Niue Assembly, and has at that poll received the support –

(i) In the case of any Bill repealing or amending or modifying or extending any of the provisions of sections 2 to 9 of the Niue Constitution Act 1974 or of Articles 1 and 69 of this Constitution or of this Article, by two-thirds of the vote validly cast; and

(ii) In any other case, a vote of the majority of the votes validly cast; and

(c) The Speaker, being satisfied that it was been passed in accordance with this Constitution and with the Standing Orders of the Assembly, has endorsed on a copy of the Bill a certificate of compliance with the requirements of this Article, and has, in the presence of the Clerk of the Niue Assembly, signed that the certificate and sealed that copy with the Seal of Niue, and inscribed thereon the date of that signing and sealing; and

(d) The Clerk of the Niue Assembly has, in the presence of the Speaker, countersigned the certificate of the copy of the Bill.

(2) A Bill which becomes law in accordance with the requirements of this Article shall be part of this Constitution and shall be described as a constitutional amendment.

(3) Subject to its provisions, a constitutional amendment shall come into force on the date of its certification and sealing.

Under the Niue Assembly Standing Orders, a Constitution Review Committee (CRC) is to carry out the review of the Constitution "as directed by the Assembly and to consider any matter relevant to the Constitution where, in the view of the Chairperson and committee, it requires a review."[61] Its meetings are open to the public, but its deliberations are closed. Once the committee reports to the assembly, then its proceedings and findings are public.[62]

In the last 51 years, the Constitution has only had two amendments: first in 1992 and the second in 2024. One might view the low number of amendments as either a sign of stability or stagnation. The author suggests that it might have been due to a lack of leadership and legal support. There have been many reports seeking amendments by the CRC over the years, but they rarely progressed past the assembly.

In 2023, a motion was presented to the assembly by Premier Dalton Tagelagi to amend principles in articles 2, 4, 21, 23, 26, 35, and 55. The motion was passed by the Niue Assembly and the matter was referred to the CRC. The CRC 2024, having considered the enormity of the task, the long time span since the last review and the limited timeframe to

61 Standing Order 116(2)(d), Government of Niue.

62 *supra* note 61, standing orders 117 (2) and (3).

complete the task, suggested reducing the amendments from eight to four. These were:

(i) Change of title from Premier to Prime Minister.
(ii) Enlargement of the cabinet by increasing the number of ministers from four to six.
(iii) Extension of the term of the Assembly from three years to four years, and
(iv) Change of reference from the Audit Office of New Zealand to the Office of the Auditor-General of New Zealand.

It was also agreed that each of the constitutional amendments be dealt with individually. That is, that there would be four Constitution Amendment Bills. The proposed amendments had also been considered by earlier CRCs. These were:

1) Change of title from Premier to Prime Minister.

In the years 1988–1989 the CRC reported overwhelming public support towards the idea of having the title of Premier changed to Prime Minister. The public sentiment at the time was warm to the idea of having a prime minister on equal footing with prime ministers of other states, especially in foreign relations. Accordingly, the CRC recommended amending the title of Premier to Prime Minister.[63] In 2000, the terms of reference of the CRC included reviewing the title of the chief minister of government.[64] In 2005, the CRC recommended amending the title of Premier to Prime Minister and Acting Premier to Deputy Prime Minister.[65] The same issue was also discussed by the CRC in 2008.[66]

2) Enlarge the cabinet by increasing the number of ministers.

In 2005, the CRC recommended increasing the number of cabinet ministers from four to six and establishing the roles of the associate minister and a deputy prime minister.[67]

3) Extend the term of the assembly from three years to four years.

In 1988–1989 and 2005, the CRC supported changing the term of the assembly from three years to five years.[68]

63 *Report of the Constitution Review Committee 1988–1989,* Niue Assembly (Government of Niue)

64 *Report of the Constitution Review Committee 2000,* Niue Assembly (Government of Niue)

65 *Report of the Constitution Review Committee 2005,* Niue Assembly (Government of Niue).

66 *Report of the Constitution Review Committee 2008,* Niue Assembly (Government of Niue).

67 *supra* note 64.

68 *supra* note 63.

4) Change the reference to Audit Office of New Zealand to the Office of the Auditor-General of New Zealand.

    The CRC in 2000 in its terms of reference included reviewing and reporting on the appropriateness of having the Audit Office of New Zealand as the Auditor for Niue.

In August 2024, the people of Niue voted in favour of two out of four proposed amendments. These were the change of title from Premier to Prime Minister and the change of the reference from the Audit Office of New Zealand to the Office of the Auditor-General. Under the two-thirds majority rule, the title of Prime Minister succeeded only in amending the Constitution but fell short of the two-thirds majority needed to change the Niue Constitution Act 1974.

After 50 years of self-government in free association with New Zealand, the leader of Niue elevated from premier to prime minister. Aside from local activities, there was no special effort to mark the 50-year relationship between the two states. With the benefit of hindsight, would it have been useful to revisit the principles of the constitutional relationship and re-evaluate what has worked and what hasn't? There is no reason why such a re-evaluation should not take place.

The challenges in relation to the free association arrangement and the continued assistance from New Zealand lie in the actual implementation of those principles. Alison Quentin Baxter stated that "although economic assistance to all associated States has overall been generous, it has been provided within a similar frame of reference as aid to independent States."[69] New Zealand has been reluctant to maintain economic and administrative assistance without close control over spending. The close control is facilitated by the New Zealand representative stationed on Niue.

She provides further that:

> the economies of scale applied to mainland communities to identify a critical mass for the purpose of allocating funds for schools, hospitals, ports, airfields and other facilities cannot be applied to the islands. Of necessity, they must to a large degree, be self-contained. Even allowing for differences in standards of living that must usually be accepted, they generally cost more per head of population to service adequately than mainland communities. Therefore, just providing the infrastructure may be disproportionately costly. And if sea or air transport is required over long distances of open ocean, safety

69 Alison Quentin-Baxter, "Sustained Autonomy – An Alternative Political Status for Small Islands?" (1994) 24 VUWLR 1, p. 4.

> requirements may make it difficult to provide this for a small population on a commercially viable basis.

The author concludes that the constitutional relationship between Niue and New Zealand has come at a cost of losing more Niueans to New Zealand, a constant battle to maintain a reasonable standard of living, and of Niue receiving the bare minimum economic and administrative support.

3.3 The Laws of Niue

The formal laws of Niue can be traced back to the 1900s. The laws passed from 1900 to 1916 were passed by the Niue Council. The laws passed from 1916 to 1959 were by the Island Council of Niue. These are in addition to laws that the governor from New Zealand could impose as a result of the annexation. That is,

> the Governor by, Order in Council, may from time to time direct that any of the laws in force in New Zealand ... shall have operation and be observed in the Islands as in his opinion are expedient for the peace, order, good government and welfare of the inhabitants.[70]

However, from October 19, 1974, all laws have been passed by the Niue Assembly.[71] Under Section 82 of the Constitution, enactments include:

(a) Any Act of the Niue Assembly and any Ordinance; and any regulation, rule, bylaw, or other instrument of the like nature made pursuant to any such Act or Ordinance;

(b) Any Act of the Parliament of New Zealand which extends to Niue as part of the law of Niue; and any Order in Council, Proclamation, regulation, rule, ministerial warrant, bylaw, or instrument of a like nature, made pursuant to any Act to which this paragraph applies, if that Order in Council, Proclamation, regulation, rule, ministerial warrant, bylaw, or other instrument extends to Niue as part of the law of Niue.

70 Cook and Other Islands Government Act 1901, No. 44, Section 2.

71 Chronological Table of Statutes Niue Laws, Tau Fakatufono-Tohi a Niue, Legislation as at December 2006, Vol. 1, xxxi. There are a few laws passed under the request and consent procedure under Article 36 of the Constitution.

The hierarchy of laws for Niue is:[72] –

(i) The Constitution.
(ii) Acts of the assembly.
(iii) Regulations.
(iv) Niuean custom.
(v) The common law of Niue.

In respect of the court decisions that have formed the common law of Niue, many of the precedents that the courts refer to are the common law of New Zealand, or sometimes of the UK. The examples are decisions dealing with injunction applications. In *Lolani v. Talagi*,[73] the court referred to the principles for granting injunctions as set out in the New Zealand case of *Klissers Farmhouse Bakeries Ltd v. Harvest Bakeries Ltd*.[74] In *Palalagi v. Talafasi*[75] the court referred to the essential purpose of an interim injunction as set out in *Roseneath Holdings Ltd v. Grieve*.[76]

There are several laws that formalize principles of Niuean custom. For example, the Domestic Fishing Act 1985 provides for marine reserves and *fono* for fishing. That Act provides that "with concurrence of the village council and or the Director, the Cabinet may by public notice declare a marine reserve, or a fono for fishing over any part of the reef of Niue waters specified in such public notice."[77] The law also prohibits illegal fishing practices for the protection of fish[78] and fishing on a Sunday. These laws stem from customary rules in relation to fishing practices.

In relation to Niuean land, the *Magafaoa* is defined as:

> the family or group of persons descended from a common ancestor, including any person who has been legally adopted into the family, who at any given time are recognized as entitled by Niuean custom to any share or interest in the alnd, and excludes a former member for the family legally adopted into some other family. Where Niuean land is owned by a single person exclusively, that person is the *Magafaoa* of the land.

72 Interpretation Act 2004, Section 5; Niue Laws, Tau Fakatufono-Tohi a Niue, Legislation as at December 2019, Vol. 2, p. 362.
73 (2016) Niue LR 873.
74 [1985] 2 NZLR 129.
75 (2014) Niue LR 697.
76 [2004] 2 NZLR 168.
77 Section 7 (1) Domestic Fishing Act 1985, Niue Laws, Tau Fakatufono-Tohi a Niue, Legislation as at December 2019, Vol. 2, 51.
78 *Ibid.*, Sections 3 and 13.

In cases where one family competes to exclude the other so as to extinguish their rights to land, the court has ruled that Niuean custom is inclusive not exclusive. In the same spirit of inclusivity, the court has ruled that a *Leveki Magafaoa* in undertaking consultations must "consult members whether they are resident in Niue or elsewhere, and that residency on the land does not give any person greater entitlement over the other members of the *Magafaoa* or a lesser obligation to consult with non-resident members."[79]

In addition to the aforementioned body of laws, the other body of laws that apply to Niue that has had an impact on modern government business is that of international treaties. Some of them are implemented in domestic law and many have not. For instance, the Taoga Niue Act 2012,[80] implements the cultural standards proclaimed under the United Nations Declaration on the Rights of Indigenous Peoples and the UNESCO Convention Concerning the Protection of the World Cultural and Natural Heritage.

Although Niue is not a member of the United Nations, it is a member of several specialized UN intergovernmental agencies. Niue is a member of all key regional intergovernmental organizations namely the Pacific Islands Forum, the Pacific Community, the South Pacific Regional Environment Programme, and the Forum Fisheries Agency, to name a few. As of late, Niue has entered into direct diplomatic relations with more than 20 countries. As of August 2024, it signed a Joint Communique with the Marshall Islands with the intention to "deepen relationships with fellow small island states and formally establish diplomatic relations with members of the Forum family."[81]

3.4 Legal Pluralism in the Context of Niue

As illustrated in the preceding discussion in this chapter, there are multiple sources of domestic law that are binding on Niue plus the influence of international law.

These multiple sources of law have created layers and levels of law which have shaped the perceptions and expectations of the Niue community towards law and justice. In the worst-case scenario, law is regarded as complex and intimidating to an ordinary Niuean person.

79 *Laifone v. Tauekipaoa* (2019) Niue LR 1317
80 Niue Laws, Tau Fakatufono-Tohi a Niue, Legislation as at December 2019, Vol 2., 439., Sections 3 and 4.
81 "Government of Niue establishes diplomatic relations with the Republic of the Marshall Islands" 2024. Media release.

In an earlier work, the author has stated that "Niuean custom has little impact on the operation of the law, although it is significant socially and at certain points is relevant in land rights matters."[82] This statement was made based on the gap between formal law, custom that is formalized in law and custom that is lived experience.

While formal laws establish the government and regulate certain activities, the majority of the people are law-abiding because of their religious beliefs and faiths. Indirectly, the belief systems have protected the customary practice of giving, sharing, nurturing, and protecting families. Every Niuean family belongs to one Christian faith or another. Covenant making and obedience to principles are voluntary. There are no offences or punishments for disobeying commandments and covenants.

Niuean society may be bound by the formal laws passed by the assembly, but there remains a disconnect between the two. Many factors contribute to this divide. Language is one; the mode of transfer is another. Formal law almost always defeats unwritten custom, although the absence of written custom does not mean it doesn't exist. It is often not understood or relied upon as a source of law. This is evident in the lack of Niuean common law principles.

However, it is interesting to note that the earlier laws of Niue prohibited the sale of land, prohibited immoral behaviour, and prohibited alcohol consumption. Currently, the law against the sale of land remains intact; de facto relationships were considered immoral in earlier laws but are lawful since the Family Relationships Act 2022.[83] The sale of alcohol for consumption is provided for under the Liquor Act 1975.[84]

In the face of existing law and the pressure to maintain a certain standard as influenced by international law, Niue is at risk of losing sight of why laws exist in the first place. The plurality of the legal system is complex; the government law office is small, there is only one law firm in private practice, the judiciary is small, courts are held only twice a year and there are insufficient qualified lawyers to assist. This has led to overburdened and overcommitted individuals in a very small and vulnerable state.

3.5 Situation of the People in the Justice System of Niue

Article 37 of the constitution provides for the establishment of a High Court as a court of record to administer justice in Niue. It has all the

82 Kahealani Sinahemana Hekau Niue, in Jennifer Corrin and Tony Angelo (eds), *Legal Systems of the Pacific, Introducing Sixteen Gems* (Cambridge: Intersentia Ltd, 2021), p. 172.

83 Niue Legislation Supplement, 2021–2024 (Wellington, New Zealand), p. 133, Section 19.

84 Niue Laws, Tau Fakatufono-Tohi a Niue, Legislation as at December 2019 (Wellington, New Zealand), Vol. 2 at 387.

jurisdiction in criminal, civil, and land to administer the law in force in Niue. The Chief Justice of the High Court is appointed by the governor-general acting on the advice of the prime minister.[85] The judges of the High Court are appointed by the governor-general acting on the advice of the minister of justice.[86] Judges cannot serve beyond 68 years of age. Their salaries are determined by Act and are a charge under the Niue Government Account.[87] Commissioners[88] of the High Court and justices of the peace[89] are appointed by the cabinet.

Several challenges exist in the current justice system. In the last 20 years since the destruction of the High Court by Cyclone Heta, Niue has not had a dedicated courthouse. The High Court sittings before a judge or the chief justice are held at a makeshift venue in available public spaces. These sittings are only held twice a year. Other sittings of the High Court on criminal matters before a commissioner and justices of the peace occur more regularly, at least once a month.

Although the judicial system is the third arm of Niue's government, the fact that there are no locally based judges, no courthouse, and a small number of lawyers on the island means that the people cannot readily access the justice system. Where they do, it might be to a limited extent. On the principle of independence of the justice system, the setup under the Constitution means that the salaries of the judges are paid for from the Niue Government Account. The expenditures under the Niue Government Account are appropriated for by the assembly. Essentially, the Public Service Commission determines the salaries of judges since they determine salaries for all.

In other matters, the socialization of law as a key aspect of Niue society has not occurred. Law is understood by a few and perceived with suspicion by many. Civic education is not taught at schools. The CRC in 1988[90] reported that:

> Education must be aimed at educating future citizens of Niue and not future citizens of New Zealand and any other country. The principles and the institutions of the State embodied under the Constitution, as well as the traditional values and customs of the Niue people must form part and parcel of school curriculum in order to imprint upon the younger generations of Niue a sense of national pride and commitment to their own country.

85 Article 42(a), Constitution of Niue, Government of Niue, 2007.
86 *supra* note 85, article 42(b).
87 *supra* note 85, article 44.
88 *supra* note 85, article 46.
89 *supra* note 85, article 51.
90 *supra* note 65, para 16.

3.6 Current Challenges Faced by Niue in the Context of Law and Justice

The challenges that Niue faces in the context of law and justice are due to several factors. The small size of the population and the drift to New Zealand in the last 50 years have severely limited the capacity to effectively build a state that is strong in the rule of law and in the administration of justice. While New Zealand citizenship has provided opportunities for many, at the same time it has weakened Niue's identity and resolve for nation building.

Fortunately, the small size of the society has meant that the island is clean and crime is minimal. But Niue could do more for itself by strengthening youth through formal education and cultural training and for its leaders to continuously review its constitution and engage in law reform. Currently, not many laws respond to the needs of the local people. More and more laws are enacted to meet regional and international obligations.

The advice of Professor R.Q. Quentin-Baxter in 1971 is useful to reflect on

> why, then, should constitutional development not wait until further progress has been made in the economic, social and educational spheres? The reason is that these other forms of development, though very important, cannot by themselves solve Niue's problems. If the small community of Niue is to have a life of its own, and to resist the drift of population it must build up its own institutions of government. These in turn can give the people of Niue the will to make progress, with New Zealand assistance in the economic, social and educational fields. Already, the basis of democratic government has been laid. The Niue Island Assembly makes the laws and controls the budget. The Executive Committee has the legal and constitutional authority to make policy. The main need is to consolidate past progress.

With 50 years' experience and looking in hindsight, there is an opportunity for Niue to continue to make adjustments in the face of its challenges.

References

Literature

Angelo, Tony and Jennifer Corrin (eds.), *Legal Systems of the Pacific, Introducing Sixteen Gems* (UK: Intersentia, 2021).

Chapman, Terry et al., *Niue: A History of the Island. University of the South Pacific and Government of Niue* (Suva, 1982).

Government of Niue, *Chronological table of Statutes, Niue Laws*, Vol 1 (2006).

Government of Niue, *Report of the Constitution Review Committee 1988–1989. Niue Assembly*, Government of Niue (1988–1989).

Government of Niue, *Report of the Constitution Review Committee 2000*. Niue Assembly, Government of Niue (2000).

Government of Niue, *Report of the Constitution Review Committee 2005*. Niue Assembly, Government of Niue (2005).

Government of Niue, *Report of the Constitution Review Committee 2008*. Niue Assembly, Government of Niue (2008).

Government of Niue, "Government of Niue Establishes Diplomatic Relations with the Republic of the Marshall Islands," (2024), Media release. available at: <https://www.gov.nu/media-releases/government-of-niue-establishes-diplomatic-relations-with-the-republic-of-the-marshall-islands>, accessed July 29, 2025.

Hekau, Kahealani Sinahemana, "Niue," in Jennifer Corrin and Tony Angelo (eds.), *Legal Systems of the Pacific, Introducing Sixteen Gems* (Cambridge: Intersentia, 2021).

Loeb, Edwin M., *History and Traditions of Niue*. Bernice P. Bishop Museum, Bulletin 32 (Honolulu, Hawaii, 1926).

Mcewen, Mary, *To Oka -- Pakeha Kaumatua, The Life of Jock McEwen* (Wellington: Riverisco Trust, 2016).

New Zealand Government, "Laws of Niue 1901," *Appendix to the Journals of the House of Representatives 1902* (1902), Session 1, A-03. available at: <https://paperspast.natlib.govt.nz/parliamentary/AJHR1902-I.2.1.2.6>.

New Zealand Government, *Appendix to the Journals of the House of Representatives* (1902). available at: <https://paperspast.natlib.govt.nz/parliamentary/appendix-to-the-journals-of-the-house-of-representatives/1902/I/169>.

Pointer, Margaret, *Niue 1774–1974: 200 Years of Contact and Change* (Otago: Otago University Press, 2015).

Quentin-Baxter, Alison, "Sustained Autonomy – An Alternative Political Status for Small Islands?" *VUWLR* 24 (1994), 1.

Quentin-Baxter, R.Q., *Report on the Constitutional Development of Niue* (Government of Niue, 1971).

Scott, Dick, *Would a Good Man Die? Niue Islands, New Zealand and the Late Mr Larsen* (Auckland: Hodder & Stoughton Ltd, Glenfield, 1993).

Tafatu, Ofa and Ianeta Joylynn Tukuitonga, "Developments to Annexation." p. 122 in Terry Chapman et al., *Niue: A History of the Island. University of the South Pacific and Government of Niue* (Suva, 1982).

United Nations General Assembly, *Resolution 1514 (XV) Office of the High Commissioner Declaration on the Granting of Independence to Colonial Countries and Peoples* (December 14, 1960).

Cases

(Citations to cases are to the reports at Niue LR and NZLR).

Klissers Farmhouse Bakeries Ltd v. Harvest Bakeries Ltd [1985] 2 NZLR 129.

Laifone v. Tauekipaoa (2019) Niue LR 1317.

Lolani v. Talagi (2016) Niue LR 873.
Palalagi v. Talafasi (2014) Niue LR 697.
Roseneath Holdings Ltd v. Grieve [2004] 2 NZLR 168.

Legislation

Cook and other Islands Government Act 1901, No. 44. available at: <https://www.nzlii.org/nz/legis/hist_act/caoiga19011ev1901n44425.pdf>.
Cook and Other Islands Act Amendment 1903 (1903), S. 4. available at: <https://www.nzlii.org/nz/legis/hist_act/caoigaaa19033ev1903n89526.pdf>.
Niue Constitution Act (1974).
Constitution of Niue (2007).
Niue Laws, Tau Fakatufono-Tohi a Niue, Legislation as at December 2019, Vol 2 (2019).
Niue Legislation Supplement (2021–2024).

4 Fragile Access to Justice in Niue

Features Revealed by the COVID-19 Pandemic

Mana Takahashi

4.1 Introduction

The novel coronavirus (COVID-19) pandemic has had an impact worldwide, including in small states such as Niue. However, the impact and resulting social changes and transformations have varied considerably according to geographical factors. Since COVID-19 was identified for the first time in December 2019, what kind of impact did it have on small countries? How did people's lives and human rights situations change? Chapter 4 considers the challenges and features of law and development faced by small island developing states (SIDS) during the COVID-19 pandemic, with the case study of Niue.

Because of their geographical characteristics, such as isolation and small size, SIDS faced unique social transformations due to the effects of the COVID-19 pandemic. Some SIDS in the Pacific region were COVID-free by the end of 2022 due to strict border control and isolation in a global society. Thus, human rights situations, necessary restrictions, and social challenges were experienced differently, and relevant policies during the pandemic were designed differently from those in larger countries and metropolises.

This research analyses the pre- and post-pandemic situations of access to justice in SIDS to clarify the transformation of society and the critical impact of the pandemic. Furthermore, it considers potential negative effects and reveals features of fragile justice in SIDS. This research focuses on Niue as the case study.

To answer the main question as to what the COVID-19 pandemic revealed in Niue with respect to challenges in law and development, three subquestions are raised: 1) How does the geographical condition of SIDS affect the transformation of society during a global pandemic, and how does it differ from that of metropolitan cities or larger countries? 2) What was the situation of access to justice in Niue after the global pandemic? 3) What kind of policy approach is feasible and appropriate for enhancing the right of access to justice in Niue?

DOI: 10.4324/9781003585688-4

4.2 Methodology and Research Framework

This research incorporates a range of different methodological approaches but mostly consists of qualitative analysis based on a socio-legal and empirical approach to examine the case of Niue. By exploring the current situation of access to justice, especially in the context of civil justice in Niue, on the basis of semi-structured interview responses with local people, government officers, and legal practitioners as well as the author's observations from fieldwork in Niue in February 2023, this research provides policy suggestions for initiatives and assistance to guarantee the right of access to justice in Niue. In this process, the talanoa methodology, which is a snowball sampling method used in the Pacific, is used to hear local voices.

The right of "access to justice" refers to the ability of individuals and businesses to seek and obtain the resolution of their legal problems through a wide range of legal and justice services, including legal aid, legal information, and formal and informal dispute resolution systems.[1] According to the Declaration of the High-level Meeting on the Rule of Law, the United Nations emphasizes the right of equal access to justice for all and reaffirms the commitment of UN member states to take all necessary steps to provide fair, transparent, effective, non-discriminatory, and accountable services.[2] Thus, the right of access to justice is a matter that extends beyond the court.[3] The law, administration, enforcement system, and dispute resolution should all be treated as legitimate. Additionally, the importance of the informal justice system is widely recognized as supplementing the limitations of the formal justice system, especially in fragile states, and the United Nations acknowledges the importance of informal justice mechanisms to ensure that vulnerable people can enjoy equal rights of access to justice.[4] The right of access to justice is defined as a principle of the rule of law and is now considered a fundamental goal to be achieved globally. It is included in the Sustainable Development Goals (SDGs) as "Goal 16: Promote peaceful and inclusive societies for sustainable development, provide access to justice for all and

1 OECD, "Access to Justice," in OECD, *Government at a Glance 2021* (Paris: OECD Publishing, 2021); United Nations and the Rule of Law, "*Access to Justice.*"

2 United Nations and the Rule of Law, *Ibid.*; United Nations General Assembly, *A/67/L.1 Declaration of the High-Level Meeting of the General Assembly on the Rule of Law at the National and International Levels* (New York: The United Nations, 2012), paras 14–15.

3 Graham Hassall, "Governance, Legitimacy and the Rule of Law in the South Pacific," in Anita Jowitt and Tess Newton Cain (eds), *Passage of Change: Law, Society and Governance in the Pacific* (Canberra: Pandanus Books, 2003), p. 65.

4 United Nations General Assembly (2012), *supra* note 2, para. 15; Tanja Chopra, and Deborah Isser, "*Access to Justice and Legal Pluralism in Fragile States: The Case of Women's Rights.*" *Hague Journal on the Rule of Law*, 4, no. 02 (2012), pp. 340–345.

build effective, accountable and inclusive institutions at all levels" and its Target 16.3, "Promote the rule of law at the national and international levels and ensure equal access to justice for all."[5] The United Nations set an indicator to measure the progress of Target 16.3, Indicator 16.3.3, which addresses civil justice, specifically measuring the proportion of the population which has experienced a dispute in the past two years and which accessed a formal or informal dispute resolution mechanism by type of mechanism.[6] However, it was not possible to measure the situation of Niue quantitatively according to this global indicator because of its small size. While Goal 16 and its Target 16.3 are applicable and should be achieved, the indicator and framework are not applicable for a country with only 1,700 people. Thus, while recognizing that the right of access to justice is significant according to the definition and global goals, a qualitative methodology is employed in this study. To identify the situation of Niue, this study refers to the instruments available to measure the degree of access to justice as well as the transition between pre- and post-global pandemics.[7] In this context, the following parameters are used: 1) legal knowledge and access to information; 2) legal aid; 3) formal court systems and services; and 4) alternative dispute resolution (ADR) mechanisms and informal justice systems. This study analyses the situation of Niue on the basis of these viewpoints in the following sections.

4.3 Features of the Justice System in Niue: How Is It Running?

Since Niue has a small community, people know each other very well. This can function as a "mutual surveillance society." One of the places that demonstrates this fact is the prison.

Niue Prison had no prisoners when the author visited in February 2023. The old prison building has no fence or gate and is not even not locked. A local person mentioned,

5 United Nations General Assembly, *A/RES/70/1 Transforming Our World: the 2030 Agenda for Sustainable Development* (New York. The United Nations, 2015), p. 25.

6 United Nations, *A/RES/71/313; E/CN.3/2022/2 Global Indicator Framework for the Sustainable Development Goals and Targets of the 2030 Agenda for Sustainable Development* (New York, 2015).

7 This study refers to several developed assessment models, but mainly the Pacific Judicial Development Programme and the *Access to Justice Assessment Toolkit* (2014). Additionally, see United Nations, *A Practitioner's Toolkit on Women's Access to Justice Programming* (2018); United Nations, Human Rights Office of the High Commissioner, *SDG-CRPD Resource Package Article 13 Indicator*.

> No one is in prison now. But even if there are prisoners, they can go to work or visit their families when they have time. The Niuean community naturally works as a monitoring system, so no one cares.[8]

How do justice systems work in Niue? The Department of Justice, Lands, and Survey under the jurisdiction of the Minister of Social Services plays a central role.[9] The department covers broad judicial and legal matters in Niue, including court services, legal consultations, procedures, and the national election.[10] Thus, the department office resembles a one-stop service centre for all justice in Niue. Regarding the judicial proceedings, the High Court has jurisdiction.[11] In addition, the commissioner and magistrates have summary jurisdiction over certain cases under the constitution and other statutes, such as small claims actions.[12]

With respect to the judicial situation in Niue, there are several problems with its operation and enforcement.

First, judicial facilities and infrastructure are limited. First, and most importantly, Niue does not have a courthouse. In 2023, the court used a conference room at the government building as a courtroom. Previously, due to Cyclone Heta, the court used a residential building and government offices as a courthouse.[13] While the department office is only the official point of contact for judicial matters for local people, the office has no proper room or space for consultation. There is a reception counter and desks and chairs for consultation in the open air; however, this makes it impossible to protect the privacy of those seeking information. Moreover, problems with the preservation and management of judicial and litigation documents exist. Land files and judicial records and documents are stored in one shipping container with aluminium filing cabinets,[14] and they are all kept on paper. None of these materials have been digitized, and no database exists. Thus, the conditions for protecting records and archives from external impacts,[15] including natural disasters, are extremely vulnerable.

8 Interview with an anonymous interviewee (1) (February 18, 2023) (Alofi, Niue).

9 Government of Niue, "Agencies."

10 Interview with Darren Tohovaka, Secretary to Justice and Registrar of the High Court of Niue (February 21, 2023) (Alofi, Niue).

11 Niue Constitution Act (1974), Art. 37(2).

12 Niue High Court Rules (1916), Rule 83, 84A.

13 Tiara T. Tukuniu, *Niue High Court Annual Report July 2015/2016–June 2018/2019* (Alofi: Niue Department of Justice, Lands, and Survey), p. 12.

14 *Ibid.*

15 In Niue, the basic rule is to record proceedings by minutes. However, it is possible that audio recordings are also kept in Niue, but to a limited extent. For example, in the Cook

Second, human resources and the capacity for judicial matters are not sufficient. One of the reasons for the lack of judicial personnel is the absence of higher education institutions in Niue that train legal professionals. Niue has only one higher education institution, the University of the South Pacific Niue campus. The University of the South Pacific offers face-to-face classes at Emalus Campus in Vanuatu and at Statham Campus in Fiji, and online courses are the only viable way to earn a law degree in Niue.[16] Currently, most of the qualified legal professionals in Niue have obtained law degrees from overseas universities and graduate schools. As of February 2023, there were four qualified legal professionals in Niue, but only two of them – one private lawyer and one public solicitor – were practising.[17] Additionally, some local people are engaged in judicial practices in Niue, including ten land commissioners and four justices of the peace; however, they have not obtained law degrees.[18] Thus, Niue generally must rely on a circuit of judges from New Zealand to conduct court trials. To compensate for this situation, civil society takes care of legal matters.[19] The Access to Justice Charitable Trust based in New Zealand dispatches pro bono lawyers to Niue to provide free legal advice to parties during court sittings.[20]

Niue has very few legal professionals but not the lowest number in the world relative to the population of the country. However, according to the Niue High Court Annual Report, the number of cases has increased, and the duration of cases has tended to increase since 2014.[21] As another critical problem, this situation places a heavy burden on judicial personnel who are engaged in legal matters, such as the registrar, secretary, and other staff at the Department of Justice, Lands, and Survey, as well as on qualified lawyers in Niue. This situation can be expected to make operations even more difficult in the future.

Third, there are no services or information systems on judicial matters that people can use appropriately and easily. The Pacific Islands Legal

---

Islands, which has a similar judicial system to Niue, there is a system of verbatim recordings by stenographers. Te Tango Tutara O The Ture (Ministry of Justice, Cook Islands), *Annual Report 2014–2015* (2015), pp. 24–25; Pacific Judicial Development Programme, *Niue Land Court Bench Book* (June 8, 2012), pp. 32–33.

16 The University of the South Pacific, "Discipline of Law."

17 *supra* note 10.

18 *Ibid.*

19 In Niue, Niue Island (Umbrella) Association of NGOs (NIUANGO) is a central body for NGOs in Niue, which is a part of the Pacific Island Association for NGOs (PIANGO). See: The Commonwealth, Pacific Island Association for NGOs (PIANGO).

20 Tukuniu, *supra* note 13, p. 21.

21 *Ibid.*, pp. 10–14.

Information Institute (PACLII)[22] exists as a database for obtaining legal information on Pacific island countries, including Niue. However, the Niue High Court does not have a website; thus, case guidelines and related information are sent by email or mail as people request.[23] The reception desk at the Department of Justice, Lands, and Survey is the only entry point for local people. Thus, obtaining appropriate information takes time and money, and this situation presents a crucial barrier to raising awareness about legal issues, procedures, and justice systems among local people. Specifically, since many Niue people are based in New Zealand, it is physically difficult for them to utilize judicial services in Niue and to obtain direct legal services locally.

Additionally, there is a financial problem: litigation tends to be expensive, and Niue does not have legal aid.[24] As mentioned above, civil society supports addressing legal matters with pro bono lawyers, but these lawyers are few and are based in New Zealand, not Niue.

With respect to the informal justice system in Niue, there is always a person in the traditional family (the *Leveki Magafaoa*, guardian, or caretaker), and that person resolves family-related problems as a mediator.[25] Community leaders and church leaders have a place in consultation, and church leaders' groups are involved in awareness-raising programmes and are gatekeepers for the proper treatment of survivors in the context of gender-based violence.[26] However, people generally prioritize consulting the *Leveki Magafaoa* or *Magafaoa* on legal matters over community leaders or church leaders.[27] Additionally, there are ADR systems, including official mediation, reconciliation, and arbitration in Niue, for which the Department of Justice, Lands, and Survey, is responsible. The providers of most ADR cases are the department staff or the registrar as well as family members who are very close to local people.

Finally, consultation services do not work properly. This issue is related to the social structure of Niue: since society as a whole is transparent about private life and operates as a mutual surveillance society, it is difficult to secure privacy. As mentioned previously, there are no proper facilities for legal consultation. Thus, although consultation services exist as a function, the reality is that they are not operated appropriately to protect the human rights and privacy of consultees. While the number was small and the available data were limited, some cases of gender-based violence

22 Pacific Islands Legal Information Institute (PACLII).

23 Tukuniu, *supra* note 13, p. 21.

24 Tukuniu, *supra* note 13, p. 17.

25 Erin Thomas, *Gender-based Violence in Niue: Challenges and Opportunities* (ICAAD, November 2021), p. 10.

26 *Ibid.*, p. 11.

27 *supra* note 10.

have been reported in Niue.[28] I asked a local woman about options for help in Niue if someone has a critical problem, such as gender-based violence or family-related problems. She answered,

> I should say, "Just go to New Zealand to rest, then come back!" That is the only solution for us.[29]

Thus, due to the social structure as well as the lack of proper facilities, it is difficult to find a place for people to consult or ask for help in Niue. However, Niue's small society also has a deterrent effect on crime. In this small society, shame and stigma are created by rumours and news spread by people and can be punishable by criminal behaviour.[30]

Regarding the judicial situation in Niue, the Secretary to Justice and Registrar of the High Court of Niue, Mr Darren Tohovaka, mentioned,[31]

> People generally respect the rule of law in Niue. Also, the number of cases of lawsuits and consultations is small, so it is manageable. Although there are many problems and limited resources, we are making the best use of existing resources and managing them.

Overall, these situations indicate that the challenges of law and justice in Niue are strongly connected to its society and its structure. From the perspective of access to justice, Niue's judicial system does not have sufficient capacity to address all matters properly.

4.4 Socio-legal Analysis of the Situation after the Global Pandemic

This section analyses the social transition and impact in Niue produced by the global pandemic. This section also demonstrates the changes, characteristics, and further challenges of access to justice and human rights situations that were revealed before and after the pandemic.

28 Erin Thomas, *Assessing Gender-based Violence in Niue* (ICAAD, 2017), pp. 11–13; Thomas (2021), *supra* note 25, pp. 14–20.

29 Interview with an anonymous interviewee (3) (February 21, 2023) (Alofi, Niue).

30 Thomas (2021), *supra* note 25, p. 12.

31 *supra* note 10.

4.4.1 *Faka Niue: The Niue Way of Responding to the COVID-19 Pandemic*

Like most Pacific island countries,[32] Niue was a COVID-19-free country for more than two years after the World Health Organization (WHO) announced on March 11, 2020 that the COVID-19 outbreak was a pandemic.[33] The first positive case of COVID-19 in Niue was found in March 2022, and there was no community transmission until July 2022.[34] In this context, most SIDS in the Pacific region decided to strictly close their borders soon after the global pandemic was declared because of their vulnerability and lack of medical capacity. The isolated geographical conditions of these SIDS contributed to preventing COVID-19 from entering their countries, and this situation made most Pacific island countries free of COVID-19 for approximately two years.

The Government of Niue announced a border closure in March 2020, and all travellers except residents and essential workers were banned from entering the country. The government responded rapidly to the pandemic: the Niue Emergency Response Plan to Coronavirus Disease 2020 was released in April 2020 to clarify national policy and action plans to mitigate the impact of COVID-19 nationwide. It included legal evidence and a legislative framework for potential restrictions and interventions as well as indicators for impact assessment.[35] Niue reopened its border in June 2022[36] but maintained strict rules to control an outbreak, including wearing masks and social distancing in public spaces. Additionally, the government requested that all travellers undergo polymerase chain reaction (PCR) tests. In February 2023, the Government of Niue announced the removal of a pre-departure test but requested that all travellers take a

32 In March 2022, only Fiji reported community transmission in the Pacific region. Tokelau was the second-last place in the world to report COVID-19 infection. Please see World Health Organization, *WHO Coronavirus (COVID-19)* Dashboard; UNICEF, *COVID-19 in the Pacific*; John Connell, *COVID-19 in the Politically Dependent Pacific Territories* (Development Policy Center, February 24, 2023).

33 World Health Organization, *Coronavirus Disease (COVID-19)*; Salote Talagi, "Political Reviews: Polynesia." *The Contemporary Pacific*, 34, no. 1, (2022), p. 200.

34 Government of Niue, *Niue Confirms Its First Positive COVID-19 Case* (Alofi, March 8, 2022). In March 2022, the number of confirmed cases worldwide was approximately 12 million, and the cumulative number of confirmed COVID-19 cases was 446.83 million. For further information, see Our World in Data, *Cumulative Confirmed COVID-19 Cases by World Region*; World Health Organization, *supra* note 33.

35 Government of Niue, *Niue Emergency Response Plan to Coronavirus Disease 2020 (COVID-19)* (Alofi, Version 4, March 17, 2022).

36 Government of Niue, "Official website of COVID-19 information for Niue: Travel to Niue."

self-rapid antigen test (RAT) on day 1 and a PCR test at the Niue Foou Hospital on day 3 after arrival[37] (Table 4.1).

Table 4.1 Key milestones of events related to the COVID-19 pandemic in Niue

Timeline	Events in Niue
March 2020	Border closure
March 2021	One-way travel bubble to NZ commenced
July 2021	The first vaccination rollout was completed (97% of eligible people vaccinated)
March 2022	First COVID-19 case confirmed
April 2022	New protocol for pre-departure test
June 2022	Border reopened (quarantine-free travel commenced)
February 2023	Pre-departure test removed
March 2023	All COVID-19 border entry requirements removed
November 2023	Air NZ restarted twice-weekly flights to Niue from Auckland

Note: Created by the author by reference to the Government of Niue, Official website of COVID-19 information for Niue.

The border closure impacted critically on people in Niue. The people of Niue hold New Zealand citizenship and because most Niuean people live in New Zealand, local people travel to New Zealand often. However, the number of regular international flights to Niue, which were run by Air New Zealand on a twice-weekly basis, was reduced to weekly or biweekly during the global pandemic.[38] According to a local woman in Niue,[39]

> Some of my family is in New Zealand, and we go back and forth with Niue. I was in Niue right before the lockdown, then returned to New Zealand. After that, I couldn't come back to Niue for nearly three years.

Border closures restricted mobility and further isolated people. Border closures affected education, especially higher education. Since Niue was a COVID-19-free country, Niue High School, and primary and secondary schools, did not need to close for a long period. However, Niue's

37 Government of Niue, *COVID-19 Update: Removal of Pre-Departure Test for Travel into Niue* (Alofi, February 7, 2023).

38 The Pacific Private Sector Development Initiative, *Pacific Tourism Sector Snapshot: Niue* (PSDI, November 2021), p. 6.

39 Interview with an anonymous interviewee (4) (February 22, 2023) (Alofi, Niue).

only institution of higher education, the University of the South Pacific (USP),[40] could not offer high-quality education for students during the pandemic because of the closure of the main campus in Fiji, and there were only limited resources on the Niue campus.[41]

Many of Niue's responses to the global pandemic, including the requested restrictions, policy implementations, and even the containment of COVID-19, were smooth. One notable fact that facilitated border opening was the high vaccination rate and the successful implementation of the vaccination rollout. According to the Government of Niue, more than 97% of eligible people were vaccinated in July 2021 with the Pfizer vaccine supplied by New Zealand, while the global rate at that time was 25.4%.[42]

Why could Niue manage COVID-19 successfully? Local people evaluated the situation as follows:

> In the beginning, everyone was very scared of the pandemic. Because Niue is a very small country and everyone knows and is close to each other, we assumed the virus would spread very quickly. I think this is the reason why everyone followed the government's policy.[43]
>
> Niue is a small country, and the communities are small too. Everyone seems to know each other, including the government people. This may also be a factor in the early and high vaccination rate.[44]

From these perspectives, the response of Faka Niue (the Niue Way) to the COVID-19 pandemic can be characterized by the following two points. First, the factors that made Niue a well-managed country during the COVID-19 pandemic were not movement restrictions, requests for self-restraint, or strict curfews but border control. Niue did not need to consider any human rights problems related to these restrictions, such as those faced by many countries worldwide during the pandemic.[45] Another issue was the lack of an alternative because the original capacity in Niue

40 The University of the South Pacific (USP) is a regional university with locations throughout countries in Oceania to meet the region's need for high-quality tertiary education, research, and policy. The university is owned and governed by 12 member countries in the Pacific region, and Niue is one of those countries.

41 The University of the South Pacific, *University Announcement* (Suva, May 18, 2021).

42 Government of Niue, *Niue Vaccination Rollout a Complete Success* (Alofi, July 14, 2023); World Health Organization, *supra* note 32; Talagi (2020), *supra* note 33, p. 201.

43 *supra* note 8.

44 Interview with an anonymous interviewee (2) (February 18, 2023) (Alofi, Niue).

45 Regarding the global problem of human rights and COVID-19, see Katharina O Cathaoir, "Human Rights in Times of Pandemics," in Morten Kjaerum, Martha F. Davis, and Amanda Lyons (eds), *COVID-19 and Human Rights* (New York: Routledge, 2021); United Nations, *COVID-19 and Human Rights: We Are All in This Together* (2020).

was low. Closed borders did represent lost opportunities for local people, such as education or employment. Second, people in Niue are very sensitive to crises; thus, they have a high acceptance of changes and new policies, and a vaccination rollout was successful. The small community and the island structure contributed to realizing this well-managed process.

It is assumed that the geographical features of SIDS influence the context of these situations. In other words, Niue's remoteness, small size, and isolation affected the responses. A lawyer and member of parliament noted the following:[46]

> Due to our smallness, people could also easily adapt. However, this view is made against the background that Niue is very isolated to begin with. That isolation has made its society resilient and adaptable. People adapt fast as a survival mechanism.

Niue's trajectory presents dimensions that are unique in global society; these are different from those of most of the world.

4.4.2 Challenges of Access to Justice in Niue

What changes have the global pandemic brought to Niue's judicial system? How were people's human rights affected? This section analyses the changes in and impact on people's situation before and after the COVID-19 pandemic on the basis of access to justice.

The Government of Niue requested that people act to avoid community infection, such as wearing masks and social distancing in public spaces, so the consultation desk at the Department of Justice, Lands, and Survey was closed during the pandemic.[47] Thus, local people had to contact the department by email or phone for initial enquiries. This situation became a critical barrier to people obtaining proper legal information. It was difficult for Niuean people overseas to obtain information without official websites or online services on legal matters.

With respect to legal aid, Niue did not have a system before the pandemic, and visiting pro bono lawyers were restricted during the pandemic. Additionally, since border closures limited litigants' travel to Niue, judicial costs and time increased. This situation made people's utilization of the judicial system and services insufficient and alienated vulnerable groups in society, who were unable to cover the cost of litigation, from proper justice systems and redress.

46 Interview with Hon. Kahealani Sinahemana Hekau, lawyer and a member of parliament of Niue (February 8, 2023) (Online).

47 Government of Niue, "Official website of COVID-19 information for Niue."

The lockdown critically affected the operation of the formal court system and legal services. Since legal professionals could not enter Niue for the court circuit during the lockdown period, court trials could not be held as usual, which caused delays.[48] The Government of Niue announced that the Niue High Court continued High Court Fixtures by accessing a judge from New Zealand via Zoom (an online platform) in February 2021.[49]

According to legal professionals in Niue:

> During the lockdown, we managed to keep up with online court sitting, but some were not covered, and it was too hard to conduct the virtual court sitting smoothly. Judges' visits from overseas resumed in November 2022.[50]
>
> Court sittings online were conducted several times during the lockdown period for three years; however, it took a much longer time. Also, there was a problem with facilities: it was very difficult to find a proper venue for an online court sitting since the internet connection is very weak in Niue. Therefore, we used a conference room of the USP Niue campus or a facility of Telecom Niue Ltd, where the internet connection is better and stable, to conduct the court sitting.[51]

A lawyer in Niue noted,[52]

> I have had court cases delayed for about two years now. In cases where there are human rights elements involved, the defendant has become severely disadvantaged.

Additionally, a problem may have arisen if the general election occurred during the lockdown. Niue does not have an overseas voting system. In-person early voting is available; however, Niueans must come to Niue to vote during the election period. Since the borders were already open during the post-pandemic general election on April 29, 2023, there was

48 Talagi (2022), *supra* note 33, p. 202; Esther Pavihi, "November Sitting of the Niue High Court with the NZ Judge - Postponed." BCN, 2022.

49 Government of Niue, *Press Release: Niue High Court Sittings 2021* (Alofi, February 1, 2021); Esther Pavihi, "Niue High Court Uses Zoom to Hear Cases with New Zealand-based Judges." BCN, 2021.

50 Interview with staff of the Department of Justice, Lands, and Survey (February 23, 2023) (Alofi, Niue).

51 *supra* note 10.

52 *supra* note 47.

no problem.[53] However, border closures and lockdowns could affect the implementation of general elections and may violate people's right to vote.

These considerations resulted in delays and increased costs and severely limited the ability to administer litigation. The parties suffered unanticipated disadvantages, and people's right to access the appropriate judicial system was also limited. ADR mechanisms and informal justice systems were within the range that can be operated in Niue. Thus, they were not critically affected. Rather, informal mechanisms were among the most valuable and significant measures used to guarantee people's rights to dispute resolution and access to justice during the pandemic.

A possible problem is that people in need or trouble might be unable to escape. In a society composed of small communities where it is difficult to protect privacy, people in trouble have nowhere to escape to if there is no appropriate consultation place for legal matters. In other words, "going to New Zealand to take a rest" did not work during the lockdown period. It is unclear how many people suffered; however, the existence of hidden demands among local people cannot be denied.

Table 4.2 presents a summary of the changes in access to justice in Niue.Overall, people's access to justice has decreased significantly since the global outbreak of COVID-19. Talagi noted that it would have been difficult to overcome the challenges that Niue faced without New Zealand's support.[54] This situation further demonstrates the vulnerability of Niue. Niue lacked alternative measures, methods, and resources to cover restrictions brought about by the pandemic because of its extremely small social structure. As a result, the already vulnerable judicial system became even weaker, leading to limited access to justice.

4.5 Recommendations for the Future to Guarantee the Right of Access to Justice in Niue

Through this observation and analysis of the situation of Niue, instability and vulnerability in the judicial system were exposed, especially after the pandemic. Some of the issues that emerged from these findings relate specifically to Niue's population composition and geographical features, including the existence of diasporas and residents in New Zealand. Sustainable measures and policies that are in line with the social context of Niue must be considered. Taken together, these findings suggest four policy recommendations along with a parameter for access to justice.

53 Government of Niue, "Premier and Cabinet."
54 Talagi (2022), *supra* note 33, p. 202.

Table 4.2 The situation of access to justice before and after the pandemic in Niue

Before the pandemic	During/after the pandemic
(1) Legal knowledge and access to Information	
• There was no website, but the Department of Justice, Lands, and Survey offered information at the reception counter.	• The reception for consultation was closed to avoid social infection. • The office asked people to enquire via phone or email. • Niue people overseas found it impossible to access the services.
(2) Legal aid	
• There was no legal aid. • Pro bono lawyers supported court sittings.	• Judicial costs became more expensive. • Pro bono lawyers from New Zealand could not visit Niue.
(3) Formal court systems and services	
• New Zealand justices visited Niue regularly to conduct court trials in person. • The venue was a conference room at the government building.	• Court sitting was conducted via Zoom. • The venue was the USP Niue campus (meeting room) due to a weak internet connection and infrastructure. • There were many delays.
(4) Alternative dispute resolution (ADR) mechanisms and informal justice systems	
• The Department of Justice, Lands, and Survey was in charge. • Family, community leaders, or church leaders sometimes dealt with legal matters as mediators, as needed.	• Not affected critically in this area. • If people needed to escape to New Zealand due to domestic problems in the closed society of Niue, it is difficult to travel overseas.

Note: Created by the author.

First, an information system to provide legal information for local people is essential. All of the Niuean legislation is publicly available from the Government of Niue. Several manuals are available.[55] However, it is important to establish a system that allows the general public to easily understand the necessary legal information. This includes simple legal interpretations, necessary procedures, guidelines, and procedural manuals. These should be prepared in both English and Niuean. It is also

55 For example, Pacific Judicial Development Programme, *Niue Land Court Bench Book*.

significant that relevant information is accessible for local people and overseas residents to address issues via the Niuean legislation. Since Niue has a small community and people are close to each other, and since there are few legal professionals, local people may need to address legal issues at the community level. Additionally, those who are not qualified as lawyers may need to volunteer to assist people in legal matters. In such cases, it would be helpful for people to have easy access to relevant legal information and guidelines. Thus, establishing a legal information system designed to increase local people's knowledge is important. Enhancing the informal justice system, including ADR mechanisms, is also important. These systems should be utilized further as self-managed mechanisms.

Second, an official legal aid system should be established in Niue. Mechanisms must be set up to overcome the barrier of litigation costs, including attorney fees and travel costs to Niue for overseas litigants. If a financial support system is difficult to establish due to capacity, it is also possible to strengthen the existing pro bono cooperation system. To enhance the current mechanisms, further collaboration or cooperation with civil society associations, including pro bono institutions overseas, should be established. It is important to develop legal services that people can use with a sense of security.

Third, to enhance the current formal court system and services, proper and fundamental facilities and infrastructure in Niue are necessary. A proper courtroom and an office for judicial work need to be established in Niue to increase the effectiveness of all legal work. Additionally, proper rooms for legal consultation should be provided, as this can protect clients' privacy, and a repository to protect legal records and archives is needed. Considering the impact of climate change, building not only physical storage but also virtual storage is desirable.

Another critical point is the vulnerability of internet connections. Since the beginning of the pandemic, this lack of infrastructure has significantly impacted the operational capacity of the judiciary and people's access to these systems. If this problem is addressed and a mechanism to conduct an online judicial system is established, it would be possible to compensate for the lack of capacity and guarantee people's access to justice. Thus, an internet-equipped courthouse that is available both in person and online should be established.

In the context of Niue, the entire structure of the judicial system should be designed to sustainably protect people's human rights because Niue is extremely vulnerable to external shocks and crises, including the global pandemic. Another serious problem may be that Niue's justice system, which was originally very vulnerable, is not well known in global society. To enhance the judicial system and access to justice, foreign aid or technical assistance is essential for Niue. In this context, it is important for aid workers who are familiar with social conditions and legal background to be involved in the rule of law. In the case of suggested infrastructure assistance, aid workers who understand their functions in a judicial context should be involved in the design. It would also be valuable to involve not only countries with similar legal systems, such as New Zealand and other Commonwealth countries but also countries and international organizations that already have know-how or experience in providing rule of law assistance, such as the United States, France, and Japan. Understanding who should be involved as aid donors and how they can cooperate with local partners in Niue is important.

4.6 Conclusion

This concluding section returns to the main research question: What did the COVID-19 pandemic reveal in Niue as a challenge in the context of law and development? This chapter explored the impact of the COVID-19 pandemic in the law and development context of SIDS and sought to gain a better understanding of the challenges of the justice system in a small island developing state and its geographical features by examining the situation of access to justice before and after the pandemic. This investigation revealed that restrictions on human rights in Niue caused by the COVID-19 pandemic differed from those that occurred in other major countries, such as movement restrictions or curfews. That is, vulnerability and geographical features such as SIDS placed limits on the right of access to a reliable justice system, and this situation was exacerbated by the COVID-19 crisis.

The findings of this study have important implications for future practice. The case study demonstrates the judicial situation and potential risks to human rights that SIDS may face. This study focused on the situation in Niue and its context of access to justice. However, this analysis has further implications. First, the potential risks and situations revealed in Niue are applicable to other SIDS or remote areas. Thus, it can be useful in considering future risks from external impacts and factors. Second, this study identified how geographical features are related to legal systems and people's rights and how they can be transformed by external shocks such as the pandemic. These perspectives can be referenced by legal practitioners as well as aid workers in rule of law assistance in the design of aid projects.

This study in Chapter 4 focused on access to justice in the field of civil justice for local people in Niue. This study was limited by a lack of information on criminology, criminal law, and its enforcement process in Niue. Thus, further research should explore this matter to obtain a comprehensive understanding of the current state and transition of the judicial system and people's access to justice in Niue.

Notwithstanding the limitations, this work provides information about Niue, especially about the challenges and transition of justice mechanisms in the pre- and post-pandemic periods, as well as valuable insights into law and development in the context of SIDS. More information about mechanisms to guarantee people's rights, related legislation, and social practices could help establish a greater degree of accuracy concerning this situation in the future.

References

Literature

Chopra, Tanja, and Deborah Isser, "Access to Justice and Legal Pluralism in Fragile States: The Case of Women's Rights." *Hague Journal on the Rule of Law* 4, no. 2 (2012), 337–58.

The Commonwealth, Pacific Island Association for NGOs (PIANGO), available at: <https://thecommonwealth.org/organisations/pacific-island-association-ngos-piango>, accessed July 27, 2025.

Connell, John, "COVID-19 in the Politically Dependent Pacific Territories." Development Policy Center, February 24, 2023, available at: <https://devpolicy.org/covid-19-in-the-politically-dependent-pacific-territories-20230224/>, accessed July 27, 2025.

Government of Niue, "Agencies." available at: <https://www.gov.nu/agencies>, accessed July 27, 2025.

Government of Niue, "Premier and Cabinet." available at: <https://www.gov.nu/premier-and-cabinet#ministers/>, accessed July 27, 2025.

Government of Niue, "Official Website of COVID-19 Information for Niue." available at: <https://covid19.gov.nu/>, accessed January 6, 2024.

Government of Niue, "Official Website of COVID-19 Information for Niue: Travel to Niue." available at: <https://covid19.gov.nu/index.php/resources/>, accessed January 6, 2024.

Government of Niue, *Niue Emergency Response Plan to Coronavirus Disease 2020 (COVID-19)* (Alofi, Version 4, March 17, 2022), available at: <https://covid19.gov.nu/wp-content/uploads/2022/03/covid-19-response-plan-update-17-march-2022-v4.pdf>.

Government of Niue, *Press Release: Niue High Court Sittings 2021* (Alofi, February 1, 2021), available at: <https://www.gov.nu/wb/media/2021/Press%20Release%201%20Feb%202021%20@%202221%20Amended%20VN%20version.pdf>.

Government of Niue, *Niue Confirms Its First Positive COVID-19 Case* (Alofi, March 8, 2022), available at: <https://www.gov.nu/wp-content/uploads/2022/03/media-release-gon-niue-confirms-its-first-covid-19-case.pdf>.

Government of Niue, *COVID-19 Update: Removal of Pre-Departure Test for Travel into Niue* (Alofi, February 7, 2023), available at: <https://www.gov.nu/wp-content/uploads/2023/02/7-february-media-release-covid-19-removal-pre-departure-testing.pdf>.

Government of Niue, *Niue Vaccination Rollout a Complete Success* (Alofi, July 14, 2023), available at: <https://gov.nu/wp-content/uploads/2021/10/media-release-gon-niue-vaccination-rollout-complete-success.pdf>.

Hassall, Graham, "Governance, Legitimacy and the Rule of Law in the South Pacific," in Anita Jowitt and Tess Newton Cain (eds.), *Passage of Change: Law, Society and Governance in the Pacific* (Canberra: Pandanus Books, 2003).

O Cathaoir, Katharina, "Human Rights in Times of Pandemics," in Morten Kjaerum, Martha F. Davis, and Amanda Lyons (eds.), *COVID-19 and Human Rights* (New York: Routledge, 2021).

OECD, "Access to Justice," in OECD, *Government at a Glance 2021* (Paris: OECD Publishing, 2021), available at: <https://www.oecd.org/en/publications/government-at-a-glance-2021_1c258f55-en.html>, accessed July 27, 2025.

Our World in Data, "Cumulative Confirmed COVID-19 Cases by World Region." available at: <https://ourworldindata.org/grapher/cumulative-covid-cases-region>, accessed July 27, 2025.

Pacific Islands Legal Information Institute (PACLII), available at: <https://www.paclii.org/>, accessed July 27, 2025.

Pacific Judicial Development Programme, *Access to Justice Assessment Toolkit* (2014), available at: <https://www.fedcourt.gov.au/pjdp/pjdp-toolkits/Access-To-Justice-Toolkit-v2.pdf>.

Pacific Judicial Development Programme, *Niue Land Court Bench Book* (June 8, 2012), available at: <https://www.paclii.org/nu/other/niue-land-courts-bench-book-2012.pdf>.

The Pacific Private Sector Development Initiative, *Pacific Tourism Sector Snapshot: Niue* (PSDI, November 2021), available at: <https://pacificpsdi.org/assets/Uploads/PSDI-TourismSnapshot-NIU2.pdf>.

Pavihi, Esther, "November Sitting of the Niue High Court with the NZ Judge -postponed." BCN (21 September, 2020), available at: <https://tvniue.com/2020/09/november-sitting-of-the-niue-high-court-with-the-nz-judge-postponed/>, accessed July 27, 2025.

Pavihi, Esther, "Niue High Court Use Zoom to Hear Cases with New Zealand Based Judges." BCN (16 February, 2021), available at: <https://tvniue.com/2021/02/niue-high-court-use-zoom-to-hear-cases-with-new-zealand-based-judges/>, accessed July 27, 2025.

Talagi, Salote, "Political Reviews: Polynesia." *The Contemporary Pacific*, 34, no. 1 (2022), 200–207.

Te Tango Tutara O The Ture (Ministry of Justice, Cook Islands), *Annual Report 2014–2015* (2015), available at: <https://www.paclii.org/ck/court-reports/2014-2015_moj_report.pdf>.

Thomas, Erin, *Assessing Gender-based Violence in Niue* (ICAAD, 2017), available at: <https://icaad.ngo/wp-content/uploads/2017/11/Assessing-Gender-based-Violence-in-Niue.pdf>.

Thomas, Erin, *Gender-based Violence in Niue: Challenges and Opportunities* (ICAAD, November 2021), available at: <https://icaad.ngo/wp-content/uploads/2021/12/Niue-GBV-Report-English-Digital-Pages-1.pdf>.

Tukuniu, Tiara T., *Niue High Court Annual Report July 2015/2016–June 2018/2019* (Alofi: Niue Department of Justice, Lands & Survey), available at: <http://www.paclii.org/nu/court-annual-reports/niuecourtsannualreport2015_2019.pdf>.

UNICEF, "COVID-19 in the Pacific." available at: <https://www.unicef.org/pacificislands/stories/covid-19-pacific>, accessed July 27, 2025.

United Nations, *A/RES/71/313; E/CN.3/2022/2 Global Indicator Framework for the Sustainable Development Goals and Targets of the 2030 Agenda for Sustainable Development* (New York, 2015), available at: <https://unstats.un.org/sdgs/indicators/Global%20Indicator%20Framework%20after%202022%20refinement_Eng.pdf>.

United Nations, *A Practitioner's Toolkit on Women's Access to Justice Programming* (2018), available at: <https://www.ohchr.org/sites/default/files/2021-08/WA2J_Consolidated.pdf>.

United Nations, *COVID-19 and Human Rights: We Are All in This Together* (2020), available at: <https://unsdg.un.org/sites/default/files/2020-04/COVID-19-and-Human-Rights.pdf>.

United Nations and the Rule of Law, "Access to Justice." available at: <https://www.un.org/ruleoflaw/thematic-areas/access-to-justice-and-rule-of-law-institutions/access-to-justice/>, accessed July 27, 2025.

United Nations General Assembly (67th sess.: 2012–2013), *A/67/L.1 Declaration of the High-Level Meeting of the General Assembly on the Rule of Law at the National and International Levels* (New York: The United Nations, 2012).

United Nations General Assembly, *A/RES/70/1 Transforming Our World: The 2030 Agenda for Sustainable Development* (New York: The United Nations, 2015).

United Nations, Human Rights Office of the High Commissioner, "SDG-CRPD Resource Package Article 13 Indicator." available at: <https://www.ohchr.org/en/disabilities/sdg-crpd-resource-package>, accessed July 27, 2025.

The University of the South Pacific, available at: < https://www.usp.ac.fj/>, accessed July 27, 2025.

The University of the South Pacific, "Discipline of Law." available at: <https://www.usp.ac.fj/discipline-of-law/>, accessed July 27, 2025.

The University of the South Pacific, "University Announcement." Suva, May 18, 2021, available at: <https://www.usp.ac.fj/covid-19-pandemic/staff-and-student-advisory/18-05-2021-university-announcement/>, accessed July 27, 2025.

World Health Organization, "WHO Coronavirus (COVID-19) Dashboard." available at: <https://covid19.who.int/>, accessed July 27, 2025.

World Health Organization, "Coronavirus Disease (COVID-19) Pandemic." available at: <https://www.who.int/europe/emergencies/situations/covid-19>, accessed July 27, 2025.

Interviews

Interview with Darren Tohovaka, Secretary to Justice and Registrar of the High Court of Niue (February 21, 2023) (Alofi, Niue).

Interview with Hon. Kahealani Sinahemana Hekau, lawyer and a member of the parliament of Niue (February 8, 2023) (Online).

Interview with Staff of the Department of Justice, Lands, and Survey (February 23, 2023) (Alofi, Niue).
Interview with an Anonymous Interviewee (1) (February 18, 2023) (Alofi, Niue).
Interview with an Anonymous Interviewee (2) (February 18, 2023) (Alofi, Niue).
Interview with an Anonymous Interviewee (3) (February 21, 2023) (Alofi, Niue).
Interview with an Anonymous Interviewee (4) (February 22, 2023) (Alofi, Niue).

Legislation

Niue Constitution Act (1974).

5 Considering the Rule of Law and Assistance in SIDS

Mana Takahashi

5.1 Introduction

Chapter 5 returns to the principal research question of the book: What kind of governance and policy initiatives are needed to ensure the rule of law and guarantee people's fundamental human rights in a vulnerable country with a small population? This research aims to answer the question by identifying the situation of law and justice and current challenges in Niue.

The preamble to the United Nations Agenda 2030 says that "Leave no one behind" is the central, transformative promise in global society.[1] The major trend in today's global society is values aimed at achieving "global goals" generated primarily from the perspectives of developed countries and the West. Given this central promise, it is necessary to "guarantee human security" for all people in the Anthropocene. Considering the global goal from this perspective, what kind of response to a SIDS, a vulnerable society, is required as the overall responsibility of the global community?

A dilemma with this approach arises. On the one hand, Pacific island countries have been on their own path towards decolonization and self-reliance since independence. On the other hand, the ideas of achieving global goals, the rule of law, the Anthropocene, and development assistance also emerged from a colonialist perspective. Furthermore, SIDS face unquestionable difficulties: they have extremely few domestic resources. Under these circumstances, how can the fundamental human rights of the people of SIDS be adequately guaranteed? How should the legitimacy of external assistance be ensured?

This chapter has two main aims. First, it reconsiders the paradigm and practices required to enhance the rule of law in the Anthropocene. This chapter recaps the theoretical framework of law and development introduced in Chapter 1 and analyses the situation in Niue from the

1 United Nations General Assembly, *A/RES/70/1 Transforming Our World: The 2030 Agenda for Sustainable Development* (New York: The United Nations, 2015), Preamble.

DOI: 10.4324/9781003585688-5

perspectives of decolonization, development, the rule of law, and the Anthropocene by unravelling each of these seemingly conflicting contexts. Second, this chapter identifies the remarkable features of SIDS in the context of law on the basis of Niue narratives and makes suggestions for rule of law assistance and the role of a global society. Since SIDS in the Pacific region have been seriously affected by climate change and other crises, a global society must consider how it should fulfil its responsibility to ensure the human rights of people in vulnerable societies. A legal and institutional framework will be needed in the context of human security.

Section 5.2 addresses the case analysis of Niue to elucidate the uniqueness and commonalities of the law and justice systems in the Pacific SIDS. Section 5.3 explores the global context and history of rule of law assistance and the experiences of rule of law assistance in the Pacific SIDS. Section 5.4 attempts to lead lessons learned for enhancing the rule of law in future SIDS on the basis of an analysis of the case of Niue. Section 5.5 concludes by identifying the limitations of this research and highlighting the implications for rule of law assistance in the future.

5.2 Case Analysis of Niue: Challenges in the Context of the Rule of Law

How can the situation of law and justice in Niue be evaluated? This section considers the case of Niue from the viewpoints of the rule of law, decolonization, and the Anthropocene.

The rule of law in Niue shows commonalities with other Pacific island countries. As noted in the previous chapters, modern laws of the South Pacific were introduced from the outside. Thus, the process of decolonization and independence that occurred after the 1960s, when most Pacific island countries had gained independence, and the way in which this influenced legislation need to be considered. Hassall noted the need to consider how independence affects capacities for governance and law and legal practices in new states.[2] In the original South Pacific societies, customs, customary laws, practices of communities, and oral orders were rooted in society and maintained order.[3] After written laws were introduced, most island countries in the South Pacific have a mixture of different kinds of legislation and constitutions; the ideology and influences of former colonial powers; and traditional unwritten rules, customs, and

2 Graham Hassall, "Governance, Legitimacy and the Rule of Law in the South Pacific," in Anita Jowitt and Tess Newton Cain (eds), *Passage of Change: Law, Society and Governance in the Pacific* (Canberra: Pandanus Books, 2003), pp. 52–53.

3 Jennifer Corrin and Vergil Narokob, *Introduction to South Pacific Law*. 5th ed. (Cambridge: Intersentia, 2022), pp. 2–3.

customary laws for social control.[4] Many countries gave them a larger role after gaining independence or self-governance, and most countries recognized them under their constitutions.[5] Niue also has a pluralistic legal structure; thus, the context of "law" in Niue means both customary laws and modern laws. This notably affects what local people consider "justice."

What does "decolonization" mean in the case of Niue? Although Kennedy has described decolonization as a process involving violence and power struggles,[6] it was extremely peaceful in Niue. In the case of Niue, it became a British protectorate in 1901 at the request of King Fataiki, who was the second king of Niue since Christianity arrived.[7] Niue was handed over to New Zealand the following year, and this lasted until October 19, 1974, when it became a self-governing state in free association with New Zealand.[8] A referendum on the 1974 constitution favoured "self-government" over independence or continued status as a New Zealand territory.[9] The 1974 written constitution thus became the supreme law of Niue and established its current status.[10] New Zealand currently has diplomatic and security responsibilities for Niue.[11] The process of Niue becoming a state in free association has been influenced by policies that promote independence, self-reliance, and decolonization, along with the will of the people of Niue.[12] Chapman sees Niue as a balanced institutional model in that it intentionally retains ties to and relies on New Zealand while increasing the effectiveness of its self-governing.[13]

However, the referendum for constitutional reform held in August 2024 revealed another perspective of Niue. While the Niue assembly and government attempted to shift the power in government, the will of the people was different, as explained in Chapter 1. In the context of SIDS,

4 *Ibid.*, pp. 2–3.

5 *Ibid.*, pp. 5–6.

6 Dane Kennedy, *Decolonization: A Very Short Introduction,* trans. Noriuyuki Osada (in Japanese). (Tokyo: Hakusuisya, 2023), pp. 13–14.

7 Tāoga Niue, "History – Tāoga."

8 Government of Niue, *Niue Legislations as at 31 December 2019*, p.v.; Caroline J. McDonald, "An Exemplary Leader?: New Zealand and Decolonization of the Cook Islands and Niue," *The Journal of Pacific History*, 3 (2020), p. 395; Tony Angelo, Elisabeth Perham, and Yi-Shen Lau, *Niue in New Zealand Legislation*, 52 Victoria University of Wellington Law Review (2021), pp. 245–246.

9 United Nations General Assembly, *A/RES/3285(XXIX). Question of Niue* (December 13, 1974).

10 RNZ Pacific, "*Niue's 50-year Journey, from Independence to Global Citizen.*"

11 The Niue Constitution Act 1974: s. 6

12 McDonald (2020), *supra* note 8, p. 395.

13 Terry Magaoa Chapman, *The Decolonisation of Niue* (Wellington: New Zealand Institute of International Affairs, 1976), p. 56.

decolonization should not necessarily result in independence. It is important to consider the need for independence as a nation-state and as SIDS. But there is the issue of a lack of governance capacity, which should be addressed. In Niue's case, fostering trust in the government and improving the government's ability would have been more important.

In the context of living in the Anthropocene, owing to exposure to the existing global crisis, Niue is fragile and vulnerable. This situation has spilled over into law and justice. Thus, not only SIDS, including Niue, but also global society as a whole should fully acknowledge its vulnerability to existing and projected crises. The law and justice sector is fragile but essential for the protection of human rights, including freedom rights and social rights, though law and justice systems are often seen as not being directly related to global crises such as climate change. Global society needs to consider how human rights can be guaranteed in legal practice to achieve the goals as a global responsibility. In terms of development, SIDS are also underdeveloped and limited in their ability to cope with everything with internal resources alone due to the inevitable factor of geographical conditions and the unequal impact of the global crisis. From the perspective of guaranteeing fundamental human rights, this situation is not desirable and should not be overlooked. Global society should understand that the global crisis can be a critical obstacle to development for these countries. Thus, after the issues and limitations of the law and justice systems are clarified, the demand for and the nature of external assistance, as well as the "appropriate use" of external resources, need to be considered.

5.3 How Should People Ensure the Operation of the Rule of Law: Rule of Law Assistance as a Countermeasure

This section explores the external assistance and efforts to enhance the rule of law and judicial conditions in SIDS. Specifically, this section examines the initiatives rule of law assistance and the experience in the Pacific island states.

5.3.1 Required Assistance and the Role of Global Society

In nations with weak social infrastructure and judicial systems, what specific efforts are being made to achieve SDGs Goal 16? In global society, rule of law assistance is a significant measure. Rule of law assistance is defined as a type of development assistance and international cooperation to design and build legal and judicial systems to establish efficient and effective justice systems and to realize the rule of law in a recipient state.

To date, many donors, including bilateral and multilateral aid agencies, have implemented rule of law assistance projects. For example, Japan has engaged in rule of law assistance since 1996, and the Japan International Cooperation Agency (JICA) has taken the lead in assisting as part of official development assistance (ODA). The forms of rule of law assistance include a wide range of areas, such as 1) legislative support; 2) development of judicial, legislative, and administrative organizations; 3) training of legal professionals and civil society; 4) development of infrastructure and facilities; and 5) research on the legal situation.[14]

The initial conception of rule of law assistance dates back to the 1960s. In the 1960s and 1970s, the United States and Europe led the Law and Development Movement (LDM), which had a goal of applying Western legal norms to Latin America and other developing countries to achieve economic growth.[15] The primary goal of the movement was to transform legal culture and institutions through educational reform and the selective transplantation of modern institutions.[16] However, implementation was ineffective as the movement was insufficiently responsive to local contexts. The United Nations also implemented some projects for legal and judicial reform in peacebuilding endeavours in this period, but these efforts were undertaken on an ad hoc basis and not wide-reaching projects.[17]

After the Cold War ended, the LDM was succeeded by the New Law and Development Movement (NLDM). The NLDM is to be distinguished from its predecessor and focuses on multidimensional legal systems, including transitional regimes, international cooperation, and conflict management.[18] The failure of the LDM and the birth of the NLDM triggered reconsideration in the international community of official views of legal reform and technical assistance. Rule of law assistance does not always aim at harmonizing the legal system under globalization. Since the law and judicial system, as well as the sense of justice, are strongly related to society, values, and traditions, the importance of designing assistance projects that are appropriate for each recipient

14 Hiroshi Matsuo, *Good Governance and the Rule of Law: A Challenge of Law and Development* (in Japanese). (Tokyo: Nippon Hyoron Sha, 2009), p. 36.

15 David M. Trubek, "The 'Rule of Law' in Development Assistance: Past, Present, and Future," in Yoshiharu Matsuura (ed.), *The Role of Law in Development Past, Present, and Future*, (Aichi: Nagoya University, 2005), pp. 1–2.

16 *Ibid.*, p. 3.

17 Calin Trenkov-Wermuth, *United Nations Justice: Legal and Judicial Reform in Governance Operations*. (Tokyo: United Nations University Press, 2010), pp. 15–16.

18 Yasunobu Sato, "The International Cooperation Law under Globalisation: Cooperation for Peace Building" (in Japanese). *Forum of International Development Studies*, 18 (2001), pp. 72–73.

society and people has been recognized. Trubek explained that through the experiences of the LDM's failure and the following rule of law movement, international donors changed development policies to stress the need for a context-specific project development model based on consultation with all stakeholders.[19] Aikyo also described rule of law assistance as a "special phenomenon in the sense that a country or international organization is directly involved in the formation of the laws of foreign country or region through the assistance."[20] Reconsidering the context of rule of law assistance demonstrates the uniqueness and features of particular aid.

The justification and implementation objectives of rule of law assistance in the 1990s were primarily economic cooperation in establishing market systems in recipient countries; however, the end of the Cold War brought an expansion of demand for legal reform as well as rule of law assistance.[21] Countries in diverse conditions, which include conflict zones and post-conflict zones and those in transition to a market economy and democracy, had demand for legal reform.[22] As global society recognized establishing the rule of law in a society as an essential element of good governance, enhancing human rights, and democratization, rule of law assistance includes a wide range of objectives, such as building democracy and good governance, peace building, maintaining order, ensuring fairness and equity, and guaranteeing human rights.

Currently, the actors engaged in rule of law assistance are not only international organizations and bilateral donors (government agencies) but also universities, research institutions, private sectors, and civil society including non-governmental organizations (NGOs). Each donor has a wide range of objectives; thus, approaches to rule of law assistance are becoming more diverse and multipolar. As Yasuda explained, rule of law assistance is an "artificial legal transplant movement between donor and recipient countries with some intention and purpose."[23] In this context, how should the current rule of law assistance be explained in terms of legitimation and goals? The diversification of objectives beyond economic growth alone, as was the initial objective of the 1990s, is related to the process of developing aid policies. Recently, they have reflected common challenges and values at the global level, as exemplified by the United Nations' Agenda 2030 and the Sustainable Development Goals.

19 Trubek (2005), *supra* note 15, pp. 11–15.

20 Masanori Aikyo, *Houseibi-shien toha nanika* (in Japanese). (Aichi: The University of Nagoya Press, 2011), p. 6.

21 Nobuyuki Yasuda, *Law and Development: A Study on Legal Systems of Asian Post-Development States* (in Japanese). (Aichi: The University of Nagoya Press, 2005), p. 327; Matsuo (2009), *supra* note 14, pp. 30–31.

22 Yasuda (2005), *Ibid*., pp. 313–315; Matsuo (2009), *supra* note 14, pp. 30–31.

23 Yasuda (2005), *Ibid*., p. 327.

5.3.2 Rule of Law Assistance in the Pacific SIDS

In the Pacific SIDS, a variety of rule of law assistance projects have been implemented.

One notable and unique example is the long-running Regional Assistance Mission to Solomon Islands (RAMSI), or Operation Helpem Fren, which was deployed from July 2003 to June 2017 in Solomon Islands.[24] As part of RAMSI, extensive rule of law assistance projects were implemented. In the multiethnic Solomon Islands, the tension between the people of Guadalcanal and Malaita intensified between 1998 and 2003. In response, the Solomon Islands government raised a request for assistance to the Pacific Islands Forum (PIF), which is a regional organization in the Pacific region. The PIF decided to implement RAMSI on the basis of the Biketawa Declaration, which established a security framework for the region. RAMSI is unique because it is not a mission under the UN umbrella, such as a UN peacekeeping operation, but rather a regional mission authorized by the PIF and implemented with regional consensus, aiming to assist in post-conflict stabilization and governance reform in Solomon Islands.[25] The mission was led primarily by Australia as the largest donor in three key areas of focus: 1) law and justice; 2) machinery of government; and 3) economic reform.[26] RAMSI was deployed on a large scale in a post-conflict society, covering a comprehensive range of areas. As a result, social order and security in Solomon Islands were dramatically restored, and social stability improved. On the other hand, there have been many criticisms of RAMSI regarding the form and effectiveness of project implementation, including its poor cost performance as a mission and weak relationship building with local people.[27] However, RAMSI is evaluated as a rare case worldwide in terms of being a regional collective action by a regional organization.

Furthermore, regional organizations in the Pacific implement various activities and offer support to enhance law and justice systems. The Pacific Islands Law Officers' Network (PILON), which is an association of senior law officers from 19 Pacific island countries and territories, plays a significant role in advancing key law and justice sectors in the region.[28]

24 Andrew Leith, "The Regional Assistance Mission to Solomon Islands," *PRISM*, 2, no. 3 (2011), 155–164; Sinclair Dinnen, "Solomon Islands—RAMSI, Transition and Future Prospects," *Security Challenges*, 8, no. 4 (2012), pp. 61–72.

25 Dinnen (2012), *Ibid.*

26 Pacific Islands Forum, "RAMSI and the Regional Spirit of Helpem Fren," Ashley Wickham, *So Near and Yet So Far* (Development Policy Center, July 3, 2013); Dinnen (2012), *Ibid.*

27 Jenny Hayward-Jones, *Australia's Costly Investment in Solomon Islands: The Lessons of RAMSI* (2013), The Lowy Institute.

28 Pacific Islands Law Officers' Network (PILON).

PILON is a network of senior officials and experts from legal institutions in the Pacific Islands region, of which the PIF is a key observer. The PIF supports PILON's activities and promotes joint efforts to strengthen the legal system in the region. PILON provides diverse guidelines, toolkits, and model laws and policies on specific issues for countries in the region, as well as a platform for sharing experiences and exchanging information on legal issues in Pacific island countries. PILON also has a legislative drafters' committee that provides technical assistance and support in drafting legislation as requested by each country. In some countries in the region, the laws are outdated, and the local experts are inexperienced owing to the lack of capacity for legislative drafting. For example, the Republic of Nauru implemented the Consolidation of Laws project to revise all of the laws of Nauru in 2021; this was the first revision since 1968.[29] In this process, the legal professionals were able to carry out their tasks, drawing on their experience in other countries and the support of PILON.[30] In this way, through the technical cooperation of the PILON Legislative Drafters' Committee, human exchange and cooperation, such as technical cooperation and the ability to apply the experience gained in another country in the Pacific region in one's own country, can be realized.

There are ways to strengthen solidarity and cooperation within the Pacific region and specific strategies for unity within the region, such as those represented by the 2050 Strategy for the Blue Pacific Continent.[31] The 2050 Strategy for the Blue Pacific Continent was developed by the PIF, which sets out the Pacific region's approach to collectively work to achieve the long-term vision and aspirations of the 2050 Strategy through seven key thematic areas, including climate change and its impacts.[32] This collective action as Pacific regionalism is critical in terms of showing the regional presence in a dialogue on global issues in general. Such cooperation at the regional level is important in the law and justice sector as well, and dialogue and cooperation among nations with cultural, geographical, and social proximity can be effective. Moreover, individual and specific responses are also necessary in the areas of law and policy, so each of these areas needs to be examined.

Legislative support projects have also been implemented to address issues specific to Pacific island countries, such as sustainable consumption

29 Pacific Islands Law Officers' Network Legislative Drafters' Committee (PLDC), *Annual Circular Edition 1* (2024), pp. 27–28.

30 *Ibid*.

31 Pacific Islands Forum Secretariat, "2050 Strategy for the Blue Pacific Continent."

32 Pacific Islands Forum Secretariat, *Forum Communique: Forty-eighth Pacific Islands Forum* (2017).

and production (SCP). Pacific island countries have limited natural resources and are vulnerable to risks such as climate change. In addition, institutions, infrastructure, and technology for waste management are underdeveloped. This situation calls for the establishment of sustainable institutions that balance environmental protection and economic activities. In response to this situation, the Secretariat of the Pacific Regional Environment Programme (SPREP) in cooperation with the JICA, the United Nations Environment Programme (UNEP), and other organizations developed a long-term strategy for comprehensive and sustainable waste management and pollution prevention and control in the Pacific islands region through 2025, entitled "Cleaner Pacific 2025 Pacific Regional Waste and Pollution Management Strategy 2016–2025."[33] Under this strategy, the rule of law assistance projects for institutional design related to SCP have been implemented. As part of the initiative, the Pacific–European Union Waste Management Programme (PacWastePlus) is a five-year regional assistance to strengthen waste and pollution management in Pacific island countries funded by the EU and implemented by SPREP.[34] PacWastePlus provided technical assistance to Pacific island countries to develop, amend, and operationalize national laws, regulations, and policy frameworks to enable sustainable and effective waste management. Specific efforts include assessing existing national legislation and governance capacity and making recommendations for needed policies, such as waste management in Kiribati and e-waste in Samoa.[35] The project also provides policy development and legislative guidelines for related issues such as waste licensing and environmental monitoring, as well as model policies for implementation.[36]

In addition to regional missions and initiatives, international organizations at the global level are providing rule of law assistance.

The Asian Development Bank (ADB) is implementing the Law and Policy Reform Program (LPR Program),[37] a technical assistance programme to support the legal system and capacity building to support sustainable development, including in Pacific island countries. Specifically, the ADB provided technical assistance for the introduction and revision

33 SPREP, *CLEANER PACIFIC 2025 Pacific Regional Waste and Pollution Management Strategy* 2016–2025 (2016).

34 PacWastePlus, "The Pacific – European Union (EU) Waste Management Programme."

35 PacWastePlus, *Assessment of Legislative Frameworks Governing Waste Management in Kiribati* (2020); PacWastePlus, *Assessment of Legislative Frameworks Governing Waste Management in Samoa* (2020).

36 PacWastePlus, *A Step-by-Step Guide to Implementation: Waste Licensing and Environmental Monitoring* (2022); PacWastePlus, *Template Policy: Waste Licensing and Environmental Monitoring Policy – Pacific Island Countries and Territories* (2022).

37 Asia Development Bank, "Law and Policy Reform Program."

of the International Arbitration Act, as well as capacity building and training of judicial officers in the region.[38]

The United Nations Development Programme (UNDP) is taking the lead in providing rule of law assistance for comprehensive policy development, including strengthening national justice systems. In Samoa, the UNDP designed the Law and Justice Sector Plan 2020–2025, which is a five-year work plan for legal reform and strengthening the law and justice sector in Samoa.[39] The project has been implemented together with local partners, including the Ministry of Justice and Courts Administration of Samoa, and the Law and Justice Sector Plan has been in place since 2012 and has been updated and reviewed every few years.[40] This initiative highlights the UNDP's long-term engagement in Samoa's law and justice sector to support a government and judicial capacity in Samoa. In the process of developing a plan, priorities, issues, and target groups in the judicial sector for each period are defined, considering the alignment of global and regional goals with Samoa's national policies.[41]

Additionally, the UNDP implemented initiatives to strengthen the justice sector in the Republic of Nauru. This initiative is part of the UNDP Nauru Accountable and Inclusive Governance (NAIG) Project, which was implemented from May 2021 to December 2024.[42] The project is funded by the Australian government on the basis of democratic values and is consistent with the National Strategy for Sustainable Development (2019–2030) in the Republic of Nauru.[43] It aims to build capacity in practice by providing training and other activities to strengthen the capacity of the Government of Nauru and the Ministry of Justice, as well as civil society organizations working in the field of human rights to address legal issues.[44]

The Republic of Nauru is a single island nation with an area of approximately 21 square kilometres and a population of approximately 12,000. In the late 1990s, the Republic of Nauru was known as a prosperous nation with the phosphate industry as its main source of foreign currency. However, it is now depleted, and the lack of major industries has left the country in a difficult economic environment. There are only

38 Asia Development Bank, "ADB Presents Overview of International Arbitration Reform in the South Pacific."

39 Government of Samoa, *Law and Justice Sector Plan 2021–2025* (2021); UNDP Cook Islands, Niue, Samoa, and Tokelau, "Samoa launches Law and Justice Sector Plan 2020–2025" (May 3, 2021).

40 Government of Samoa (2021), *Ibid.*, pp. 16–17.

41 Government of Samoa (2021), *Ibid.*, pp. 30–32.

42 UNDP, *UNDP Nauru Accountable and Inclusive Governance (NAIG) Project.*

43 Republic of Nauru, *National Sustainable Development Strategy 2019–2030* (2019).

44 UNDP Pacific Office, "New Initiative to Strengthen Nauru Justice Sector."

limited domestic resources, and the country faces problems caused by the effects of climate change, such as land erosion due to sea level rise and lack of freshwater resources. The current project focuses on areas of justice and governance, but it is designed from the perspective of "the whole-of-island approach," which comprehensively addresses the complex intertwined social issues in Nauru and explores what can be effective in realizing sustainable development.[45] This approach is unique to small island countries, where society as a whole is compact and people are deeply connected. From the perspective of aid effectiveness, aid methods that consider the social context are needed. Moreover, the ways in which the situation in the Republic of Nauru will change in the future need to be examined for a long-term perspective.

Various other forms of bilateral assistance in the justice sector have also been implemented. The major donor countries in the Pacific region are Australia and New Zealand, which have geographic proximity and a common law system.

Australia identified cooperation towards achieving SDGs Goal 16 and the rule of law as one of the priority areas in its ODA strategy. Approximately 10% of the total ODA budget is allocated to the achievement of Goal 16, and 25% of all implemented projects are in the area of justice and governance in Pacific island countries.[46]

Australia has a wide range of projects throughout the Pacific, particularly in Melanesian countries such as Papua New Guinea, Solomon Islands, Fiji, and Nauru, in areas strengthening the courts, building the capacity of judicial institutions, and strengthening security and police structures. Additionally, the law and justice area of RAMSI was taken over by the Solomon Islands Justice Program (SIJP) (2014–2021) and followed the Australia Solomon Islands Partnership for Justice (ASIPJ) (2022–2025) as a bilateral aid project of Australia after RAMSI's official withdrawal in 2017. The Australian government has continuously implemented a series of projects to strengthen and build capacity in the justice sector in Solomon Islands.[47]

New Zealand has also implemented bilateral assistance projects in the justice sector in Samoa, Tonga, Nauru, and Vanuatu, as well as throughout the Pacific. To achieve effective governance, increase transparency, and build responsible and competent justice systems in the Pacific region,

45 UNDP Pacific Office, "A 'Whole-of-Island' Approach: Flipping the Script on the Way We Do Development in Nauru."

46 Australian Government, Department of Foreign Affairs and Trade. *Australian Official Development Assistance Statistical Summary 2021–22* (2022), pp. 17–19.

47 Abt Associates, *Solomon Islands Justice and Governance Program Evaluation* (2020); Mana Takahashi, "Lessons from Project Transition Experiences of Australian Law and Justice Assistance in Solomon Islands," *Journal of Australian Studies*, 31 (2018), pp. 1–22.

these projects have strengthened the institutions and procedures of courts and justice systems, supported the capacity building of legal professionals, and strengthened legal information systems.[48] For example, the Government of New Zealand implemented rule of law assistance projects in the Cook Islands. The Cook Islands is in a state of free association with New Zealand, which is the same status as Niue. The Cook Islands is a nation of 15 islands spread over 2 million square kilometres of ocean. Owing to such geographical conditions, the Cook Islands faces a serious problem of access to justice, especially for people on remote islands.[49] Accordingly, New Zealand has conducted training for justices of the peace in the Cook Islands. Justices of the peace are important for Pacific island countries in common law legislation, where resources and experts are scarce, to resolve legal issues and maintain public order. Achieving capacity building of the justices of the peace and increasing the number of them in the local community through training and Train the Trainer programmes has led to outcomes such as independence in dispute resolution within the Cook Islands, provision of judicial services in remote areas with local languages, and enabling the handling of a wide variety of legal issues.[50] Additionally, the Government of New Zealand has provided technical assistance with legislative drafting to support the legislative capacity of the Cook Islands.[51] New Zealand collaborated with Australia on working for women's rights and on gender-related issues and with other bilateral donors to identify focus areas for enhancing law and justice capacity.[52]

In recent years, other donors have begun to embark on rule of law assistance on Pacific islands. China, for example, implemented construction projects of the Courthouse (the building of the Ministry of Justice) and National Police Headquarters as part of a Chinese Buildings Renovation Project in the Cook Islands with a NZ$ 11.94 million budget.[53] While it is important to have the physical facilities, many criticisms exist because such initiatives do not consider the size and social conditions of the small island country, and are too large to manage.[54] The approaches of traditional and emerging donors seem different, and there appear to be differences in methods even among bilateral donors. Thus,

48 Clear Horizon, *MFAT Support to Pacific Justice Sector 2010–2020 Evaluation Report* (2021), p. 5.
49 *Ibid.*, pp. 43–44.
50 *Ibid.*, pp. 41–44.
51 *Ibid.*, pp. 42–43.
52 *Ibid.*, p. 43.
53 AIDDATE, "Chinese Government Provides RMB 70 Million Grant."
54 For example, see RNZ, "China Provides Funds to Refurbish Buildings on Rarotonga." (January 17, 2018).

consideration of the social context of recipients and inter-donor coordination in assistance, which are fundamental elements of aid, will play an increasingly important role.

The following points regarding rule of law assistance to the Pacific SIDS are suggestions for future initiatives.

First, the pluralistic legal systems of Pacific island countries require a more general approach to the legal systems (such as informal legal systems and customary law) that the local people rely on in practice. Most approaches to rule of law assistance have focused on formal dispute resolution mechanisms and judicial systems which have been heavily influenced by the former colonial powers as donors until now. Given decolonization, people's more specific legal challenges, and a need for improved access to justice, further consideration is required as to how individual legal issues can be resolved in practice. In this context, more diverse perspectives, not limited to common law legal systems and donors from former colonial powers but also donors with experience in implementing rule of law assistance projects, may need to be included.

Second, aid projects should be provided that are appropriate to the social context and size of the small island states. In recent years, extremely large-scale projects that did not match the size and needs of the recipient countries have been implemented in the Pacific SIDS at the will of the donors, but this approach does not necessarily lead to long-term sustainable development for the recipient society and people.[55] This fact applies not only to rule of law assistance but to aid projects in general. Just as there are criticisms against long-term interventions such as RAMSI, the donor side must always consider avoiding unnecessary lengthening of a period, scaling up projects, implementing, and establishing a sustainable mechanism that is functional in a society facing the unique environment and risks of small island states.

5.4 Lessons Learned from Niue to Enhance the Rule of Law in SIDS

In the Anthropocene, what does a justice system for "Leave no one behind" in SIDS look like? What kinds of policy approaches are necessary to enhance the rule of law? What lessons can be drawn from Niue's experience? On the basis of the situation in Pacific small island countries and the case of Niue, this section considers the responsibilities and necessary measures that global society should fulfil in the future. As mentioned

55 For example, Mana Takahashi, "The Role of the Quad in the Context of Human Security: Can the Quad Become a Good Neighbor of the Blue Pacific?," *Journal of Human Security Studies*, 13, no. 1 (2024), pp. 1–20.

in previous chapters, Niue is receiving technical support in the law and justice sector from New Zealand, including drafts and legal expert dispatch at the request of Niue. It is important for the justice sector to be self-sustaining and have ownership in the sector by each country. On the other hand, an extremely small country such as Niue has limitations in terms of domestic resources. Thus, making good use of external resources is inevitable.

In the Anthropocene, the geographical structure of SIDS and their compact societies may be beneficial in response to crises. As described in Chapter 4 in the case of the COVID-19 pandemic in Niue, vaccination coverage was extremely high. In a compact and well-connected society, solidarity among the society as a whole is more likely to emerge, and efficient management becomes possible. Moreover, a vulnerable society can respond flexibly and quickly to crises because people are more sensitive to these crises.

However, SIDS are more vulnerable in areas that rely on external resources. Thus, consideration of the increased impact and types of risks that may arise in the Anthropocene is needed. The law and justice system is inevitably vulnerable to inadequate domestic resources and capacities, which can have a significant impact because the area relies on human resources such as legal experts. The impact of the COVID-19 pandemic is an example of how the situation regarding people's access to justice worsened. In areas where external resources are essential, tangible measures are needed to ensure the guarantee of people's rights, such as the development of infrastructure and the establishment of alternative means of access. In the Anthropocene, having the governance capacity to work with global society and to weather external crises is essential. In addition to the management and governance capacity of the government, society itself should have the capacity for solidarity, the ability to formulate and implement policies, ensure transparency to the public, disclose and provide information, and engage in activities related to promoting the understanding of policies. Establishing such good governance in SIDS is important for managing the nation independently with limited domestic resources. Traditional values such as customs, informal rules, and local languages that are deeply rooted in Pacific SIDS need to be considered in governance.

What are the responsibilities required of global society? The respective circumstances of SIDS should be considered, and an approach tailored to individual contexts is necessary. For the Pacific SIDS, in addition to the characteristics of their national judicial systems, providing rule of law assistance from the perspective of "decolonization" and response to the Anthropocene is important. In other words, a recipient society needs to establish an independent system that can guarantee the fundamental human rights of local people in any environment while respecting the values, customs, and ideas rooted in that society.

Ironically, as indicated in the Introduction, the idea of rule of law assistance itself seems to be a colonial approach. With respect to the legitimacy of external aid to the Pacific SIDS facing the dilemma of decolonization and resource scarcity, what is significant is how to think about the "ways and means" of assistance, based on the premise that external assistance is essential because of the inevitable condition of geographical vulnerability. From this perspective, the following three points should be noted as necessary policy approaches in the future.

First, developing a proper infrastructure related to law and justice systems is essential. However, it must be sized appropriately for the social context of SIDS and be sustainably managed and maintained. Specifically, facilities for dispute resolution and consultation, as well as facilities to store judicial documents, are needed. Infrastructure is also needed to ensure that people on remote islands have access to appropriate judicial services. As the case of Niue shows, in areas where court circuits are in place, for example, during the COVID-19 pandemic, the small island nation became isolated and unable to operate a proper judicial system because people could not travel due to border closures and restrictions. Additionally, the migration of people across borders is common in the Pacific SIDS. Thus, a system that can be accessed by those both on and off the islands needs to be implemented. Complementing these aspects is the need for infrastructure, such as internet access, sufficient to provide information and services online. This infrastructure would protect the people's rights in the event of a global risk.

Second, there needs to be a mechanism to provide information that will enable people to understand their legal system. As mentioned previously, in Pacific island countries where resources are scarce, specialists have been providing dispute resolution and judicial services by way of a circuit court, and experts from New Zealand are responsible for some of the work in Niue. In several countries, national and international experts are involved in judicial affairs. Thus, professionals engaged in judicial services, including pro bono, need to have a mechanism for understanding the culture and laws of the people of the country or region concerned. Additionally, human migration and the effects of climate change are significant in Pacific island countries and are expected to increase. Under these circumstances, it will be necessary to train people in individual societies to use judicial services appropriately, and to provide necessary legal information and legal education.

Finally, donor diversity must be ensured. In other words, an appropriate legal system needs to be designed with the involvement of a wide range of donors, not just former colonial powers. Aid projects should be implemented as "horizontal" linkages rather than "vertical" relationships reminiscent of former colonial powers and their colonies. While societies are unique, there are commonalities among Pacific island countries in terms of geography, decolonization processes, and pluralistic structures of law. In addition to providing guidelines and model laws, such as those already in place, it may be possible to transfer technology into instruments for designing laws and policies. These could be particularly useful in the design of laws and policies in areas of global issues, such as climate change, human migration, and human rights issues. Furthermore, the sharing of experience and best practices in rule of law assistance within the Pacific region would be valuable for the future implementation of effective assistance projects.

In today's global society, in addition to these approaches, the rationale and purpose for the implementation of the rule of law assistance need to be reconsidered. The commitment of global society not only to economic growth and development but also to the ways in which aid projects can comprehensively contribute to the achievement of global goals such as Agenda 2030 and the SDGs in the Anthropocene need to be reaffirmed. It is also important to incorporate the perspective of building a global society of "Leave no one behind" into the objectives of rule of law assistance. On the basis of this goal, the implementing donors, their involvement, and the justification for their assistance must be clearly stated. It may be necessary to design an aid model to realize human rights guarantees while being aware of the Anthropocene and the global context, the sustainable development goals to be achieved, and the linkages between them.

5.5 Conclusion

This chapter has examined the situation of law and justice and current challenges in Niue, based on a perspective of decolonization, the Anthropocene, and development. The chapter also explored the influence of rule of law assistance experiences in the Pacific SIDS to consider potential and required approaches by global society.

Since Niue was the main focus of the book, the individual context of each unique society was not examined in detail. Thus, generalizing about the overall trend of the law and justice situations and related assistance in the Pacific region is difficult. Future studies should be conducted to examine other societies in the Pacific SIDS to enable comparative analysis. A major limitation of this study is the lack of sufficient evaluation of the effectiveness of legal assistance. Rule of law assistance tends to be a long-term project due to the nature of the sector. This is because these projects take a long period for the new systems and structures brought about by external assistance to take effect. The transformation and changes in society should be monitored for several decades. In this context, the question raised by this study for the future is what effects will be seen when rule of law assistance projects on Pacific islands are evaluated from a long-term perspective.

Despite the limitations, this study provides suggestions for approaches to the rule of law assistance needed in the Anthropocene. As globalization intensifies and new global risks from increasingly human-made activities arise, the demands to provide rule of law assistance projects have changed. Aid providers and policy makers in global societies should not simply modify their approaches but reconsider their objectives and legitimacy. In the context of law and justice assistance, donor organizations should also design a tangible blueprint for law and justice systems as well as legal reform in a recipient country, with comprehensive viewpoints including the recipient's needs; global standards; and the social context, culture, and economic conditions.

Taken together, these findings suggest a role for global society in promoting the rule of law as a responsibility and how initiatives and approaches can be effectively accomplished.

This study has elucidated the poorly understood situation of Niue and the Pacific SIDS. SIDS are often forgotten, and their information is often inadequate. While Agenda 2030 stated the global goals, it may be difficult for global society to understand the situation of SIDS, owing to their small size and features. In particular, the judicial and human rights situation is difficult to grasp when the social context and the position of the state are not considered. This planet is not composed solely of developed countries, and global goals should not be set from the perspectives of those countries. Identifying and understanding the situation of these nations, including the difficulties and limitations of their societies, is a significant first step in considering global goals. All nations, both large and small, are equally valuable. Society certainly exists in Niue and other small island states, and people live there. Traditions, culture, language, and customs have been created there, and the dignity of the people living there should be respected. As stated in the preamble to Agenda 2030, global society must not forget these facts.

References

Literature

Abt Associates, *Solomon Islands Justice and Governance Program Evaluation* (2020), available at: <https://www.dfat.gov.au/sites/default/files/solomon-islands-governance-and-justice-program-evaluation-final-report.pdf>.

AIDDATE, "Chinese Government Provides RMB 70 Million Grant." available at: <https://china.aiddata.org/projects/69560/>, accessed July 27, 2025.

Aikyo, Masanori, *Houseibi-shien toha nanika (in Japanese)* (Aichi: The University of Nagoya Press, 2011).

Angelo, Tony, Elisabeth Perham, and Yi-Shen Lau, "Niue in New Zealand Legislation," *Victoria University of Wellington Law Review*, 52 (2021), 245–284.

Asia Development Bank, "ADB Presents Overview of International Arbitration Reform in the South Pacific." available at: <https://lpr.adb.org/resource/overview-international-arbitration-reform-south-pacific?utm_source=chatgpt.com>, accessed July 27, 2025.

Asia Development Bank, "Law and Policy Reform Program." available at: < https://lpr.adb.org/?utm_source=chatgpt.com >, accessed July 27, 2025.

Australian Government, Department of Foreign Affairs and Trade, *Australian Official Development Assistance Statistical Summary 2021–22* (2022), available at: <https://www.dfat.gov.au/sites/default/files/australias-official-development-assistance-statistical-summary-2021-22.pdf>.

Chapman, Terry Magaoa, *The Decolonisation of Niue* (Wellington: New Zealand Institute of International Affairs, 1976).

Clear Horizon, *MFAT Support to Pacific Justice Sector 2010–2020 Evaluation Report* (2021), available at: <https://www.mfat.govt.nz/assets/Aid-Prog-docs/Evaluations/2021/Strategic-Evaluation-MFAT-Support-to-Pacific-Justice-Sector-Evaluation-Report-2010-2020.pdf>.

The Commonwealth, Pacific Island Association for NGOs (PIANGO), available at: <https://thecommonwealth.org/organisations/pacific-island-association-ngos-piango>, accessed July 27, 2025.

Corrin, Jennifer, and Vergil Narokobi, *Introduction to South Pacific Law* (5th ed. Cambridge: Intersentia, 2022).

Dinnen, Sinclair, "The Solomon Islands—RAMSI, Transition and Future Prospects," *Security Challenges*, 8, no. 4 (2012), 61–72.

Government of Niue, *Niue Legislations as at 31 December 2019*, available at: <https://www.gov.nu/wp-content/uploads/2022/03/niue_laws_vol1_il2022.pdf>.

Government of Samoa, *Law and Justice Sector Plan 2021–2025* (2021), available at: <https://www.mof.gov.ws/wp-content/uploads/2022/08/Law-Justice-Sector-Plan-2021-2025.pdf>.

Hassall, Graham, "Governance, Legitimacy and the Rule of Law in the South Pacific," in Anita Jowitt and Tess Newton Cain (eds.), *Passage of Change: Law, Society and Governance in the Pacific* (Canberra: Pandanus Books, 2003).

Hayward-Jones, Jenny, *Australia's Costly Investment in Solomon Islands: The Lessons of RAMSI* (2013), The Lowy institute. available at: <https://www.lowyinstitute.org/sites/default/files/hayward-jones_australias_costly_investment_in_solomon_islands.pdf>.

Kennedy, Dane, *Decolonization: A Very Short Introduction,* trans. Noriuyuki Osada (in Japanese) (Tokyo: Hakusuisya, 2023).

Leith, Andrew, "The Regional Assistance Mission to the Solomon Island," *PRISM*, 2, no. 3 (2011), 155–164.

Matsuo, Hiroshi, *Good Governance and the Rule of Law: A Challenge of Law and Development (in Japanese)* (Tokyo: Nippon Hyoron Sha, 2009).

McDonald, Caroline J., "An Exemplary Leader?: New Zealand and Decolonization of the Cook Islands and Niue," *The Journal of Pacific History*, 3 (2020), 394–417.

Pacific Islands Forum, "RAMSI and the regional spirit of Helpem Fren." available at: <https://forumsec.org/publications/ramsi-and-regional-spirit-helpem-fren>, accessed July 27, 2025.

Pacific Islands Forum, "2050 Strategy for the Blue Pacific Continent." available at: < https://forumsec.org/2050 >, accessed July 27, 2025.

Pacific Islands Forum Secretariat, *Forum Communique: Forty-Eighth Pacific Islands Forum* (2017), available at: <https://www.forumsec.org/wp-content/uploads/2018/02/Final_48-PIF-Communique_2017_14Sep17.pdf>.

Pacific Islands Law Officers' Network (PILON), available at: <https://pilonsec.org/ >, accessed July 27, 2025.

Pacific Islands Law Officers' Network Legislative Drafters' Committee (PLDC), *Annual Circular Edition 1* (2024), available at: <https://pilonsec.org/wp-content/uploads/2024/11/5130-PLDC-Annual-Circular-%E2%80%93-Edition-1-2024-V4-SCREEN.pdf>.

PacWastePlus, "The Pacific – European Union (EU) Waste Management Programme." available at: <https://pacwasteplus.org/>, accessed July 27, 2025.

PacWastePlus, *Assessment of Legislative Frameworks Governing Waste Management in Kiribati* (2020), available at: <https://kiribati-data.sprep.org/system/files/waste-legislation-Kiribati.pdf>.

PacWastePlus, *Assessment of Legislative Frameworks Governing Waste Management in Samoa* (2020), available at: <https://library.sprep.org/sites/default/files/2021-03/waste-legislation-Samoa.pdf>.

PacWastePlus, *A Step-by-Step Guide to Implementation: Waste Licensing & Environmental Monitoring* (2022), available at: <https://pacwasteplus.org/wp-content/uploads/2022/05/Waste-Licensing-and-Environmental-Monitoring_A-Step-by-Step-Guide-to-Implementation.pdf>.

PacWastePlus, *Template Policy: Waste Licensing and Environmental Monitoring Policy – Pacific Island Countries and Territories* (2022), available at: <https://pacwasteplus.org/wp-content/uploads/2022/05/Template-Policy-1.pdf>.

Republic of Nauru, *National Sustainable Development Strategy 2019–2030* (2019), available at: <https://naurufinance.info/wp-content/uploads/2020/07/Final-NSDS-2019-2030.pdf >.

RNZ, "China Provides Funds to Refurbish Buildings on Rarotonga." (17 January, 2018), available at: <https://www.rnz.co.nz/international/pacific-news/348327/china-provides-funds-to-refurbish-buildings-on-rarotonga>, accessed July 27, 2025.

RNZ Pacific, "Niue's 50 year Journey, from Independence to Global Citizen." available at: <https://www.rnz.co.nz/news/pacific/531299/niue-s-50-year-journey-from-independence-to-global-citizen>, accessed July 27, 2025.

Sato, Yasunobu, "The International Cooperation Law under Globalisation: Cooperation for Peace Building (in Japanese)." *Forum of International Development Studies*, 18 (2001), 71–83.

SPREP, *CLEANER PACIFIC 2025 Pacific Regional Waste and Pollution Management Strategy 2016–2025* (2016), available at: <https://sustain

abledevelopment.un.org/content/documents/commitments/1326_7636_commitment_cleaner-pacific-strategy-2025.pdf>.

Takahashi, Mana, "Lessons from Project Transition Experiences of Australian Law and Justice Assistance in Solomon Islands," *Journal of Australian Studies*, 31 (2018), 1–22.

Takahashi, Mana, "The Role of the Quad in the Context of Human Security: Can the Quad Become a Good Neighbor of the Blue Pacific?," *Journal of Human Security Studies*, 13, no. 1 (2024), 1–20.

Tāoga Niue, "History – Tāoga." available at: <https://taoganiue.nu/history/>, accessed July 27, 2025.

Trenkov-Wermuth, Calin, *United Nations Justice: Legal and Judicial Reform in Governance Operations* (Tokyo: United Nations University Press, 2010).

Trubek, David M., "The 'Rule of Law' in Development Assistance: Past, Present, and Future," in Yoshiharu Matsuura (ed.), *The Role of Law in Development Past, Present, and Future* (Aichi: Nagoya University, 2005).

United Nations General Assembly, *A/RES/3285(XXIX). Question of Niue* (December 13, 1974).

UNDP, *UNDP Nauru Accountable and Inclusive Governance (NAIG) Project*, available at: <https://undpngddlsprod01.blob.core.windows.net/pdc/Nauru%20Governance%20ProDoc%20Final.docx.pdf >.

UNDP Cook Islands, Niue, Samoa and Tokelau, "Samoa Launches Law & Justice Sector Plan 2020–2025" (May 3, 2021). available at: <https://www.undp.org/samoa/news/samoa-launches-law-justice-sector-plan-2020-2025>, accessed July 27, 2025.

UNDP Pacific Office, "New Initiative to Strengthen Nauru Justice Sector." available at: <https://www.undp.org/pacific/press-releases/new-initiative-strengthen-nauru-justice-sector>, accessed July 27, 2025.

UNDP Pacific Office, "A 'Whole-of-Island' Approach: Flipping the Script on the Way We Do Development in Nauru." available at: <https://www.undp.org/pacific/blog/whole-island-approach-flipping-script-way-we-do-development-nauru>, accessed July 27, 2025.

United Nations General Assembly, *A/RES/70/1 Transforming Our World: The 2030 Agenda for Sustainable Development* (21 October, 2015).

Wickham, Ashley, *So Near and Yet So Far* (Development Policy Center, July 3, 2013), available at: <https://devpolicy.org/ramsi-so-near-and-yet-so-far-20130703-2/>, accessed July 27 2025.

Yasuda, Nobuyuki, *Law and Development: A Study on Legal Systems of Asian Post-Development States (in Japanese)* (Aichi: The University of Nagoya Press, 2005).

Legislation

Niue Constitution Act (1974).

Constitution of Niue (2019).

6 Conclusion

Kahealani Sinahemana Hekau

6.1 Implications for the Future

As discussed in earlier chapters, the context of Niue's law and justice system depends on and serves a very small population. Its small population and isolation are some of its unique challenges that could threaten its ability to survive in this increasingly interconnected and fast-paced world. For this reason, the law and justice system is overburdened and underserved.

It is suggested that Niue should re-evaluate its law and justice systems, build an educated and informed population base in order to not just survive, but to thrive in the next decade. There is ongoing work on law consolidation.

Its leaders now have the benefit of hindsight and could learn from past mistakes and missed opportunities. Although the last 50 years of constitutional relationship with New Zealand may not have yielded any outstanding achievements, there is opportunity to improve in the coming years.

To conclude, a five-year strategic implementation plan is suggested. The plan should build on the development pillar on governance under the Niue National Integrated Strategic Plan 2021–2026.[1] It should include a vision and three main goals. The goals should provide the current situation and targets.

The above should be carried out at:

(1) Political level;
(2) Administrative level;
(3) Local government level; and
(4) Family and home level.

Each of the above levels should have an objective followed by actions over a five-year period. Each should have a quarterly monitoring and

1 Niue National Integrated Strategic Plan.

DOI: 10.4324/9781003585688-6

compliance scoreboard to encourage performance. This should be supported by an annual law and justice forum for sharing progress and review.

Hanei e tutonuhia mo e tofi he tagata Niue![2]

Reference

Niue National Integrated Strategic Plan, available at: <https://policy.asiapacificenergy.org/sites/default/files/Niue%20National%20Strategic%20Plan.pdf>.

2 For this is the privilege and responsibility of a Niuean person.

Index

Page numbers in *italics* indicate figures while page numbers in **bold** indicate tables.

Made in the USA
Las Vegas, NV
19 September 2026

ac81cc66-c741-429b-a365-f8040a329a63R01